FLAT STANLEY

Invisible Stanley

Invisible Stanley

Text copyright © 1996 by Jeff Brown
Illustrations by Macky Pamintuan, copyright © 2009 by HarperCollins Publishers
All rights reserved.

Published in agreement with the author, c/o BAROR INTERNATIONAL, INC., Armonk, New York, U.S.A. through Danny Hong Agency, Seoul, Korea.

ISBN 979-11-91343-62-5 14740

Longtail Books

FLAT STANLEY

Invisible Stanley

by Jeff Brown
Pictures by Macky Pamintuan

For Robert Brown
—J.B.

CONTENTS

Prologue

Stanley Lambchop spoke into the darkness above his bed. "I can't sleep. It's the rain, I think."

There was no **response** from the bed across the room.

"I'm hungry, too," Stanley said. "Are you awake, Arthur?"

"I am now," said his younger brother.

"You woke me."

Stanley **fetch**ed an apple from the kitchen and ate it by the bedroom window. The rain had **worsen**ed.

"I'm still hungry," he said.

"Raisins*. . . **shelf** . . ." **murmur**ed
Arthur, half asleep again.

Crash! came **thunder. Lightning flash**ed.

Stanley found the little box of raisins on
a shelf by the window. He ate one.

Crash! Flash!

Stanley ate more raisins.

Crash! Flash!

Arthur **yawn**ed. "Go to bed. You can't
be hungry still."

"I'm not, actually." Stanley got back into
bed. "But I feel sort of . . . oh, *different*, I
guess."

He slept.

★ raisin 건포도.

Where Is Stanley?

"Breakfast is ready, George. We must wake the boys," Mrs. Lambchop said to her husband.

Just then, Arthur Lambchop called from the bedroom he shared with his brother.

"Hey! Come here! Hey!"

Mr. and Mrs. Lambchop smiled, **recall**ing another morning that had begun like

this. An **enormous bulletin board**, they **discover**ed, had fallen on Stanley during the night, leaving him unhurt but no more than half an inch* thick. And so he had remained until Arthur blew him round again, weeks later, with a bicycle **pump**.

"Hey!" The call came again. "Are you coming? Hey!"

Mrs. Lambchop **held firm view**s about good manners and correct speech. "**Hay** is for horses, not people, Arthur," she said as they entered the bedroom. "As well you know."

"Excuse me," said Arthur. "The thing is, I can *hear* Stanley, but I can't *find* him!"

★ inch 길이의 단위 인치. 1인치는 약 2.54센티미터이다.

Mr. and Mrs. Lambchop looked about the room. A shape was **visible beneath** the **cover**s of Stanley's bed, and the **pillow** was **squash**ed down, as if a head **rest**ed upon it. But there was no head.

"Why are you **staring**?" The voice was Stanley's.

Smiling, Mr. Lambchop looked under the bed but saw only a **pair** of **slipper**s and an old tennis ball. "Not here," he said.

Arthur put out a hand, **exploring**. "**Ouch**!" said Stanley's voice. "You **poke**d my nose!"

Arthur **gasp**ed.

Mrs. Lambchop stepped forward. "If I may . . . ?" Gently, using both hands, she felt about.

A **giggle** rose from the bed. "That *tickles!*"

"Oh, my!" said Mrs. Lambchop.

She looked at Mr. Lambchop and he at her, as they had during past great surprises. Stanley's flatness had been the first of these. Another had come the evening they discovered a young genie,★ Prince Haraz, in the bedroom with Stanley and Arthur, who had **accidental**ly **summon**ed him from a lamp.

Mrs. Lambchop **drew a deep breath.** "We must **face** facts, George. Stanley is now invisible."

"You're *right!*" said a **startle**d voice from the bed. "I can't see my feet! Or my **pajamas**!"

"Darnedest✷ thing I've ever seen," said Mr. Lambchop. "Or *not* seen, I should say. Try some other pajamas, Stanley."

★ **genie** 지니. 아라비아 신화에 나오는 병이나 램프 속에 사는 요정.
✷ **darnedest** '몹시 놀라운' 또는 '터무니없는'이라는 뜻의 'damnedest'를 순화한 표현.

Stanley got out of bed and put on different pajamas, but these too **vanish**ed, **reappear**ing only when he took them off. It was the same with the shirt and **trouser**s he tried on next.

"**Gracious!**" Mrs. Lambchop shook her head. "How are we to keep *track* of you, **dear**?"

"I know!" said Arthur. Un**tying** a small red balloon, a **party favor**, that **float**ed above his bed, he gave Stanley the **string** to hold. "Try this," he said.

The string vanished, but not the
balloon.

"There!" said Mrs. Lambchop. "At least
we can tell, **approximate**ly, where Stanley
is. Now let's all have breakfast. Then,
George, we must see what Dr. Dan **makes**
of this."

Dr. Dan

"What's that red balloon doing here?"
asked Dr. Dan. "Well, **never mind**.
Good morning, Mr. and Mrs. Lambchop.
Something about Stanley, my nurse says.
He's not been taken flat again?"

★ **ventriloquist** 복화술사. 인형을 안고 연극을 하면서 입을 움직이지 않고
전혀 다른 목소리를 내어 인형이 말하는 것처럼 느끼게 하는 사람.

"No, no," said Mrs. Lambchop. "Stanley has remained round."

"They mostly do," said Dr. Dan. "Well, let's have the little **fellow** in."

"I am in," said Stanley, standing directly before him. "Holding the balloon."

"Ha, ha, Mr. Lambchop!" said Dr. Dan. "You are an excellent ventriloquist!* But I **see through** your little **joke**!"

"What you see through," said Mr. Lambchop, "is Stanley."

"**Beg pardon**?" said Dr. Dan.

"Stanley became in**visible** during the night," Mrs. Lambchop explained. "We are quite **unsettle**d by it."

"**Headache**?" Dr. Dan asked Stanley's balloon. "**Throat sore? Stomach upset**?"

"I feel fine," Stanley said.

"I see. Hmmmm . . ." Dr. Dan shook his head. "**Frankly, despite** my long years of **practice**, I've not **run into** this before. But one of my excellent **medical** books, *Difficult and Peculiar Cases* by Dr. Franz Gemeister, may help."

He took a large book from the **shelf** behind him and looked into it.

"Ah! '**Disappear**ances,' page 134." He found the page. "Hmmmm . . . Not much here, I'm afraid. France, 1851: a Madame Poulenc **vanish**ed while eating bananas in the rain. Spain, 1923: the Gonzales twins, age eleven, became invisible after eating fruit salad. **Lightning** had been **observed**. The most recent case, in 1968, is Oombok, an Eskimo* **chief**, last seen eating **canned** peaches during a **blizzard**."

Dr. Dan returned the book to the shelf.

"That's it," he said. "Gemeister **suspect**s a **connection** between bad weather and fruit."

"It **storm**ed last night," said Stanley. "And I ate an apple. Raisins, too."

"There you are," said Dr. Dan. "But we must **look on the bright side**, Mr. and Mrs. Lambchop. Stanley seems perfectly healthy, **except** for the **visibility factor**. We'll just **keep an eye on** him."

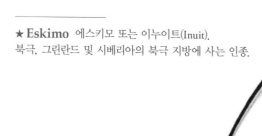

★ **Eskimo** 에스키모 또는 이누이트(Inuit).
북극, 그린란드 및 시베리아의 북극 지방에 사는 인종.

"Easier said than done," said Mr. Lambchop. "Why do his *clothes* also disappear?"

"Not my **field**, I'm afraid," said Dr. Dan. "I **suggest** a **textile specialist**."

"We've kept you long enough, Doctor," Mrs. Lambchop said. "Come, George, Stanley—Where *are* you, Stanley? Ah! Just hold the balloon a bit higher, **dear**. Good-bye, Dr. Dan."

By dinnertime Mr. and Mrs. Lambchop and Arthur had become quite sad. The red balloon, though useful in **locating**

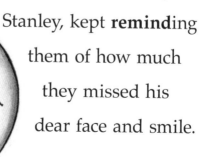

Stanley, kept **remind**ing them of how much they missed his dear face and smile.

But after dinner Mrs. Lambchop, who was **artistic**ally **talented**, **replace**d the red balloon with a pretty white one and got out her watercolor paints.* Using four colors and several **delicate brush**es, she painted an excellent **likeness** of Stanley, smiling, on the white balloon.

Everyone became **at once** more **cheerful**. Stanley said he felt almost his old self again, especially when he looked in the mirror.

★ **watercolor paint** 수채 물감. 안료를 수용성 전색제로 갠 그림 물감.

The First Days

The next morning Mrs. Lambchop wrote a note to Stanley's teacher, **tie**d a stronger **string** to his balloon, and sent him off to school.

"Dear Miss Benchley," the note said. "Stanley has **unexpected**ly become invisible. You will find the balloon a useful **guide** to his **presence. Sincerely,** Harriet

Lambchop."

Miss Benchley spoke to the class. "We must not **stare** at where we suppose Stanley to be," she said. "Or **gossip** about his **state**."

Nevertheless, word soon **reach**ed a newspaper. A **reporter** visited the school and his story appeared the next day.

The **headline** read: SMILING STUDENT: "ONCE YOU SAW HIM, NOW YOU DON'T!" **Beneath** it were two photographs, a Before and an After.

The Before, taken by Miss Benchley a week earlier, showed a smiling Stanley at his desk.

The After, taken by the reporter, showed only Stanley's desk and his smiley-face balloon **bob**bing above it. The story **include**d a statement by Miss Benchley that Stanley was in fact at the desk and, to the best of her **knowledge**, smiling.

Mr. and Mrs. Lambchop bought several copies of the paper for **out-of-town** friends. Her colorful balloon **artwork** lost something in black and white, Mrs. Lambchop said, but **on the whole** it had photographed well.

Arthur said that "Invisible Boy's Brother" would have been an interesting picture, and that Stanley should **suggest** it if the reporter came around again.

* * *

Being invisible offered **tempt**ations, Mr.
and Mrs. Lambchop **warn**ed, but Stanley
must **resist** them. It would be wrong to
spy on people, for example, or **sneak** up on
them to hear what they were saying.

But the next Saturday afternoon, when
the Lambchops went to the movies, it was
Arthur who could not resist.

"Don't buy a seat for Stanley," he
whispered at the ticket window.* "Just
hide his balloon. Who'd know?"

"That would be **deceitful**, dear," said
Mrs. Lambchop. "Four seats, please," she
told the ticket lady. "We want one for our

★ **ticket window** 매표소.

coats, you see."

"Wasn't *that* deceitful, sort of?" Arthur asked as they went in.

"Not in the same way," said Mr. Lambchop, **tuck**ing Stanley's balloon beneath his seat.

Just as the film began, a very tall man sat directly in front of Stanley, **block**ing his view. Mr. Lambchop took Stanley on his **lap**, from which the **screen** was easily seen, and the people farther back saw right through him without knowing it. Stanley greatly enjoyed the show.

"See?" said Arthur as they went out. "Stanley didn't even *need* a seat."

"You have a point," said Mr. Lambchop, whose legs had **go**ne **to sleep**.

In the Park

It was Sunday afternoon. Arthur had gone to visit a friend, so Mr. and Mrs. Lambchop **set out** with Stanley for a nearby park. The streets were **crowd**ed, and Stanley carried his balloon to **lessen** the **risk** of being **jostle**d by people hurrying by.

Near the park they met Ralph Jones, an old **college** friend of Mr. Lambchop's.

"Always a **treat run**ning **into** your family, George!" said Mr. Jones. "The older boy was flat once, I **recall**. You had him **roll**ed up. And once you had a **foreign lad** with you. A prince, yes?"

"What a memory you have!" said Mr. Lambchop, recalling the young genie who had been with them at the time.

"How are you, Ralph?" said Mrs. Lambchop.

"Stanley? Say hello to Mr. Jones."

"**Take care!**" said Mr. Jones. "That balloon is **float**ing—hmmmm . . . Just where *is* Stanley?"

"Holding the balloon," Stanley said. "I got in**visible** somehow."

"Is that so? First flat, now invisible." Ralph Jones shook his head. "Kids!

Always one thing or another, eh, George? My oldest needs **dental** work. Well, I must run! **Remember** me **to** that prince. Prince Fawzi Mustafa Aslan Mirza Melek Namerd Haraz, as I recall."

"A truly *remarkable* memory," said Mrs. Lambchop as Mr. Jones walked away.

By a **field** in the park, the Lambchops found a bench on which to **rest**.

On the field, children were **racing** bicycles, round and round. Suddenly, shouts rose. "**Give up**, Billy! . . . Billy's no good! . . . Billy, Billy, **silly** Billy, he can't ride a bike!"

"That must be Billy," said Mrs. Lambchop. "The little **fellow** so far behind the rest. Oh, **dear**! How he **teeter**s!"

Stanley remembered how nervous he had been when he was learning to ride and how his father had **steadied** him. Poor Billy! If only . . . I'll do it! he thought, and tied his balloon to the bench.

When Billy came round again, Stanley **dart**ed onto the field. **Taking hold of** the teetering bicycle from behind, he began to run.

"Uh-oh!" said little Billy, surprised to be **gain**ing speed.

Stanley ran harder, keeping the bicycle steady. The **pedal**s rose and fell, faster and faster, then faster still.

"**Yikes**!" cried Billy.

Stanley ran as fast as he could. Soon

they passed the boy riding just ahead, then
another boy and another! Not until they
had passed all the others did Stanley, now
out of breath, let go.

"Wheeee!" Billy shouted, and went
round once more by himself.

"You win, Billy!" shouted the other
boys. "How did you get so good? . . . And
so *suddenly!* . . . You sure had us **fool**ed!"

Stanley got his breath back and returned to Mr. and Mrs. Lambchop on the bench.

"Too bad you missed it, Stanley," said Mr. Lambchop, pretending he had not guessed the truth. "That teetery little boy—he rode very well suddenly."

"Oh?" said Stanley, pretending also. "I wasn't paying **attention**, I guess."

Mr. Lambchop gave him a little **poke** in

the **rib**s.

Half an hour passed, and Mrs. Lambchop
worried that they might be sitting too
long in the sun. In Stanley's **present state**,
she said, over-**tan**ning would be difficult
to **detect**.

Just then, a young man and a pretty girl
strolled past, **hand in hand**, and **halt**ed in
a **grove** of trees close by.

"That is Phillip, the son of my dear
friend Mrs. Hodgson," Mrs. Lambchop
said. "And the girl must be his **sweetheart**,
Lucia. Such a sad story! They are in love
and Phillip wants very much to **propose**
marriage. But he is too shy. He tries and
tries, Mrs. Hodgson says, but each time

his **courage** fails. And Lucia is too **timid** to **coax** the proposal from him."

Mr. Lambchop was not the least bit shy. "I'll go introduce myself," he said. "And **pop** the question for him."

"No, George." Mrs. Lambchop shook her head. "Lucia must hear the words from Phillip's own **lips**."

An idea came to Stanley.

"Be right back!" he said, and ran to the grove in which the young couple stood. Once beside them, he stood very **still**.

". . . nice day, Lucia, don't you think?" Phillip was saying. "Though they say it may rain. Who knows?"

"You are quite right, I'm sure, Phillip," the girl replied. "I do **value** your opinions about the weather."

"You are kind, very kind." Phillip **trembled** a bit. "Lucia, I want to ask . . . I mean . . . Would you . . . **Consent**, that is . . ." He **gulped**. "What a pretty dress you have on!"

"Thank you," said Lucia. "I like your necktie. You were saying, Phillip?"

"Ah!" said Phillip. "Right! Yes! For some time now, dear Lucia . . . My dearest wish . . . Oh, my! I want . . ." He **bit** his lip. "Look! A dark cloud, there in the west! It may rain **after all**."

"I hope not." Lucia seemed close to tears. "I mean, if it rained . . . Well, we might get wet."

This is *very* **boring**, Stanley thought.

The **conversation** grew even more boring. Again and again Phillip failed to **declare** his love, **chatter**ing instead about the weather, or the look of a tree, or children playing in the park.

"I want to ask, dear Lucia," Phillip began again for perhaps the twentieth time, "if you will . . . That is . . . If you . . . If . . ."

"Yes?" said Lucia, also perhaps for the twentieth time. "*What*, Phillip? *What* do you wish to say?"

Stanley **lean**ed forward.

"Lucia . . . ?" said Phillip. "Hmmm . . . Ah! I . . ."

"*Marry me!*" said Stanley, making his voice as much like Phillip's as he could.

Lucia's eyes opened wide. "I *will*, Phillip!"

she cried. "Of course I will marry you!"

Phillip looked as if he might **faint**. "What? Did I—? You *will*?"

Lucia hugged him, and they kissed.

"I've proposed at last!" cried Phillip. "I can **hardly** believe I spoke the words!"

You didn't, Stanley thought.

Mr. and Mrs. Lambchop had seen the lovers **embrace**. "Well done, Stanley!" they said when he returned to their bench, and several more times on the way home.

Mrs. Hodgson called that evening to **report** that Phillip and Lucia would soon be **wed**. How wonderful! Mrs. Lambchop said. She had **glimpse**d them in the park just that afternoon. Such a handsome **pair**! So much in love!

Stanley **tease**d her. "You said never to **sneak** up on people or **spy** on them. But I did today. Are you mad at me?"

"Oh, very angry," said Mrs. Lambchop, and kissed the top of his head.

The TV Show

Arthur **was** feeling **left out**. "Stanley always gets to have interesting **adventure**s," he said. "And that newspaper story was just about him. Nobody seems interested in me."

"The best way to draw **attention**, dear," said Mrs. Lambchop, "is by one's **character**. Be kindly. And fair. **Cheerful**ness is much

admired, as is **wit**."

"I can't manage all that," said Arthur.

Mrs. Lambchop spoke **private**ly to Stanley. "Your brother is a bit **jealous**," she said.

"When I was flat, Arthur was jealous because people **stare**d at me," Stanley said. "Now they can't see me at all, and he's jealous again."

Mrs. Lambchop **sigh**ed. "If you can find a way to **cheer** him, do."

The very next day an important TV person telephoned Mr. Lambchop.

"Teddy Talker here, Lambchop," he said.

"**Host** of the **enormous**ly popular TV show, *Talking with Teddy Talker*. Will Stanley appear on it?"

"It would please us to have Stanley *appear* anywhere at all," Mr. Lambchop said. "People can't see him, you know."

"I'll just say he's there," said Teddy Talker. "Speak to the boy. Let me know."

Stanley said that he did not **particular**ly care to go on TV. But then he remembered about cheering up Arthur.

"All right," he said. "But Arthur, too. He likes to tell **joke**s and do magic **trick**s. Say we'll *both* be on the show."

Arthur was very **pleased**, and that evening the brothers planned what they would do. The next morning Mr.

Lambchop told Teddy Talker.

"Excellent plan!" said the TV man. "This Friday, yes? Thank you, Lambchop!"

"Welcome, everybody!" said Teddy Talker that Friday evening from the **stage** of his TV show. "Wonderful guests tonight! **Including** an invisible boy!"

In the front **row**, **applaud**ing with the **rest** of the **audience**, Mr. and Mrs. Lambchop thought of Stanley and Arthur, now waiting in a **dress**ing room **backstage**. How excited they must be!

The other guests were already seated on the sofa by Teddy Talker's desk. He **chat**ted first with a lady who had written a book about sausage, next with a tennis

champion who had become a rabbi,* then with a very pretty young woman who had won a beauty **contest**, but planned now to **devote** herself to the **cause** of world peace.

★ **rabbi** 랍비. 유대교의 율법학자를 이르는 말. '나의 스승, 나의 주인'이라는 뜻이다.

50

At last came the **announce**ment that began the Lambchop plan.

"Invisible Stanley has been **delay**ed but will be here shortly," Teddy Talker told the audience. "**Meanwhile**, we are **fortunate** in having with us his very **talented** brother!"

Protests rose. "Brother? . . . A *visible* brother? . . . Drat!* . . . Good thing we got in free!"

"Ladies and gentlemen!" said Teddy Talker. "**Mirth** and magic with Arthur Lambchop!"

Arthur stepped out onto the stage wearing a **smart** black **magician's** **cape**

Mrs. Lambchop had made for him and carrying a small box, which he placed on Teddy Talker's desk.

"Hello, everybody!" he said. "The box is for later. Now let's have fun! Heard the story about the three holes in the ground?" He waited, smiling. "**Well**, well, well!"

Two people laughed, but that was all.

"I don't understand," said a lady sitting behind Mr. and Mrs. Lambchop.

Mr. Lambchop turned around in his seat. "A 'well' is a hole in the ground," he said. "'Well, well, well.' Three holes."

"Ah! I see!" said the lady.

"A **riddle**, ladies and gentlemen!"

★ **drat** 제기랄! 젠장!

cried Arthur. "Where do kings keep their **armies**?"

"Where?" someone called.

"In their **sleevies**!*" said Arthur.

Many people laughed now, including the lady who had missed the first joke. "I got that one," she said."

"A mind-reading trick!" Arthur announced. He **shuffle**d a **deck** of cards and let Teddy Talker draw one.

"Don't let me see it!" he said. "But look at it! Picture it in your mind! I will **concentrate**, using my magic powers!" Arthur closed his eyes. "Hmmm . . . hmmm . . . Your card, sir, is the four of

---

★**sleevies** 팔(arm)이 있는 곳은 소매(sleeve)이기 때문에 군대(armies)가 있는 곳은 sleevies라고 농담하고 있다.

hearts!*"

"It is!" cried Teddy Talker. "It *is* the four of hearts!"

Voices rose again. "**Incredible**! . . . He can read minds? . . . So young, too! . . . Do that one again, **lad**!"

"Certainly!" said Arthur.

But he had used a false deck in which *every* card was the four of hearts, and the audience would surely guess if that card was named again. Fortunately, the brothers had thought of this. Backstage, Stanley **tie**d his balloon to a chair.

Arthur now shuffled a real deck of

★**hearts** 트럼프 카드 팩은 스페이드(spades), 하트(hearts), 다이아몬드 (diamond), 그리고 클럽(clubs)이 표시된 카드로 구성되어 있다. 그 중 하트는 빨간색 하트 모양이 그려진 것이다.

cards, then called for a **volunteer**. When an **elderly** gentleman came up onto the stage, Stanley **tiptoe**d out to stand behind him. The audience applauded the volunteer. How **peculiar** this is! Stanley thought. Hundreds of people looking, but not one can see me!

"Draw a card, sir!" said Arthur. "Thank you! Keep it hidden! But picture it in your mind!" Again closing his eyes, he pretended to be thinking hard.

A quick **peek** showed Stanley that the volunteer held the ten of clubs.* He tiptoed over to **whisper** in his brother's ear.

★ **clubs** 카드 팩 가운데 검은색 클로버(clover)의 모양이 그려진 카드를 가리킨다.

Arthur opened his eyes. "I have it. The card is . . . the ten of clubs!"

"Yes! **Bravo**!" cried the old gentleman. The audience **clap**ped hard as he returned to his seat.

Mr. Lambchop smiled at the lady behind him. "Our son," he said.

"So **clever**!" said the lady. "What *will* he do next?"

Mrs. Lambchop **drew a deep breath**. That morning Stanley and Arthur had borrowed a **pet** frog from the boy **next door**. What came next, she knew, would be the most **daring** part of the evening's plan!

"Ladies and gentlemen!" said Arthur. "A new kind of magic! Arthur Lambchop—

that's me!—and Henry, the Air-Dancing Frog!"

He lifted Henry from the box on Teddy Talker's desk and held him up. Henry, who appeared to be smiling, wore a little white shirt with an H on it, also made by Mrs. Lambchop.

"Fly, Henry!" cried Arthur. "Fly out and stand **still** in the air!"

Stepping forward, Stanley took Henry from Arthur's hands and ran to the far side of the stage. There he stopped, holding the frog high above his head. Henry **wriggle**d his legs.

"**Amazing**!" shouted the audience. "Who'd believe it? . . . That's some frog! . . . What keeps him up there?"

"**Circle**, Henry!" Arthur **command**ed. "Circle in the air!"

Stanley walked **rapid**ly in circles, **sway**ing Henry as he went.

The audience was **tremendous**ly **impress**ed. "What a fine magician! . . .

Mind reading *and* frog flying! . . . You don't see that every day!"

Pretending to control Henry's flight, Arthur kept a finger pointed as Stanley **swoop**ed the frog all about the stage. "Whoops!" cried Teddy Talker as Henry flew above his desk. On the long sofa, the sausage writer and the tennis rabbi and the beauty-contest winner **duck**ed down. Even Mr. and Mrs. Lambchop, who knew the secret of Henry's flight, thought it an amazing **sight**.

At last, to great **applause**, Arthur took Henry into his own hands and returned him to the little box.

Stanley tiptoed off to get his smiley-face balloon. The plan now called for Teddy

Talker to announce the arrival of the
invisible boy and introduce him.

But Arthur had stepped forward again.

"Thank you for cheering me," he told
the audience. "But I have to say something.
That first mind-reading trick, I really
did do that one. But the second trick . . .
Actually, I can't read minds at all. And the
flying frog, he—"

Voices rose. "Can't read minds?" . . .
"We've been lied to?" . . . "The *frog* was
lying?" . . . "Not the frog, stupid!" . . .
"Wait, he's not done!"

"Please! Listen!" said Arthur. "It
wouldn't be fair to let you think I did
everything by myself. I had a helper! For
the second trick, he saw the card and told

me what it was. And Henry . . . Well, my helper was **whoosh**ing him in the air!"

By now the audience was **terribly confuse**d. "Who?" . . . "What helper?" . . . "It was just a regular frog?" . . . "But *some* frogs fly!" . . . "No, **squirrel**s, not frogs!" . . . *"Whooshing?"*

Arthur **went on**. "My brother, Stanley, helped me! He fixed it for me to be on this show! He's a really nice brother, and I thank him a lot!"

Teddy Talker had **sprung** to his feet. "Ladies and gentlemen! May I now **present** a very special guest, who has been here **all along**! The invisible boy! Stanley Lambchop!"

Stanley came onto the stage, carrying

his smiley-face balloon. Arthur put out

his hand, and the audience could tell

that Stanley had taken it. There was

tremendous applause.

The brothers **bow**ed again and again, Stanley's balloon **bob**bing up and down. Arthur's smile was **plain** to see, and Mr. and Mrs. Lambchop, as they applauded, thought that even the balloon's painted smile seemed brighter than before.

"I have two children myself," said the lady behind them. "Both entirely visible and without **theatrical flair**. We are a very *usual* family."

"As are we," said Mr. Lambchop, smiling. "Mostly, that is."

Arthur left the stage, and Stanley sat on the sofa between the sausage writer and the beauty-contest winner and answered Teddy Talker's questions. He had no idea *how* he became invisible, he said, and it wasn't actually a great **treat** being that way, since he often got **bump**ed into and had to keep **remind**ing people he was there. After that, Teddy Talker thanked everyone for coming, and the show was over.

Back home, Arthur felt the evening had gone well.

"I got lots of applause," he said. "But maybe it was mostly because of what Stanley did. I shouldn't be too proud, I guess."

"**Poise** and good humor **contribute** greatly to a performer's success," said Mrs. Lambchop. "You did well on both those **count**s. Return Henry in the morning, dear. Time now for bed."

The Bank Robbers

Mr. Lambchop and Stanley and Arthur
were watching the evening news on TV.

". . . more **dreadful scandal** and
violence tomorrow," said the **newscaster**,
ending a **report** on national **affairs**. "Here
in our fair city another bank was robbed
today, the third this month. The unusual
robbers—"

"Enough of **crime**!" **Bustling** in, Mrs. Lambchop **switch**ed **off** the TV. "Come to dinner!"

Stanley supposed he would never know how the robbers were unusual. But the next afternoon, while **stroll**ing with his father, he found out. On the way home they passed a bank.

"I must **cash** a **check**, but it is very **crowd**ed in there," said Mr. Lambchop. "Wait here, Stanley."

Stanley waited.

Suddenly, cries rose from within the bank. "Lady bank robbers! Just like they said on TV!" . . . "I laughed when I heard it!" . . . "Me, too!"

Two women in dresses and **fancy** hats,

one **stout** and the other very tall, ran out of the bank, each with a money bag in one hand and a **pistol** in the other.

"Stay in there!" the stout woman called back into the bank, her voice high and **scratch**y. "Don't anyone run out! Or else . . . **Bang**! Bang!"

"Right!" shouted the tall woman, also in an **odd**, high voice. "Just because we are females doesn't mean we can't **shoot**!"

Being in**visible** won't **protect** me if **bullet**s go flying about! Stanley thought. He looked for a place to hide.

An empty **Yum-Yum** ice cream **van** was parked close by and he jumped into it. His balloon still **float**ed outside the van, its **string** caught in the door, but he did not **dare** to **rescue** it. **Scrunch**ing down behind **cardboard barrel**s **mark**ed CHOCOLATE YUM, STRAWBERRY YUM, and YUM CRUNCH, he **peek**ed out.

An **alarm** was ringing inside the bank, and shouts rose again. "Ha! Now you're in trouble!" . . . "The police will come!" . . . "Put that money back where you found it, ladies!"

Then Stanley saw that the two robber women were running toward him, carrying the money bags. They were stopping! They were getting into the Yum-Yum van!

Scrunching down again, he **held his**

breath.

The robbers were in the van now, close to where he hid. "Hurry up!" said the stout woman in a surprisingly deep voice. "These shoes are killing me!"

The tall woman opened the YUM CRUNCH barrel, and Stanley saw that it was empty. Then both robbers **pour**ed **packet**s of money from their bags into the barrel and put the **lid** back on.

Stanley could **hardly** believe what he saw next!

The robbers threw aside their fancy hats and **tug**ged off **wig**s. And now they were un**dress**ing, pulling their dresses over their heads!

They were *men*, Stanley **realize**d, not

women! Yes! **Underneath** the dresses they wore white ice-cream-man pants, with the legs **roll**ed up, and white Yum-Yum shirts!

"Whew! What a **relief**, Howard!" The stout robber **kick**ed **off** his women's shoes and put on white **sneaker**s.

"They'll never catch us now, Ralph!" said the tall one.

The robbers unrolled their **trouser** legs and threw their female clothing into another empty barrel, the one marked CHOCOLATE YUM. Then they jumped into the front seats, the tall man driving, and the van **sped** off.

Behind the barrels, Stanley held his breath again. This **pair** was too **clever** to be caught! They were sure to **get away**!

No one would **suspect** two Yum-Yum

men of being the lady—But the van was

slowing! It was stopping!

Stanley peeked out again.

A police car **block**ed the road and two

policemen stood beside it, **inspect**ing cars

as they passed by. In a moment they were

at the Yum-Yum van.

"A bank got robbed," the first

policeman told the driver. "By two

women. You ice-cream **fellow**s seen any **suspicious**-looking females?"

"My!" The tall man shook his head. "More and more these days, women **fill**ing **role**s once played by men. **Bless** 'em, I say!*"

Beside him, the stout man said **hastily**, "But bank robbing, Howard, that's *wrong*."

The second policeman looked into the back of the van. "Just ice cream here," he told his partner.

The **trickery** is working! Stanley thought. How can I . . . ? An idea came to him. **Reach**ing out, he **flip**ped the lid off the CHOCOLATE YUM barrel.

★ **I say** 아이구! 어머나! 놀람이나 충격 등을 나타내는 표현.

"**Loose** lid," said the second policeman. "Better **tighten**— Hey! This barrel is full of female clothes!"

"Oh!" The tall robber made a sad face. "For the **needy**," he said. "They were my **late** mother's."

Stanley flipped the lid off the YUM CRUNCH barrel and the packets of money were **plain** to see!

"Your mother was a **mighty** rich woman!" shouted the first policeman, drawing his pistol. "Hands up, you two!"

As the robbers were being **handcuff**ed, another police car drove up. Mr. Lambchop jumped out of it.

"That balloon, on that van!" he shouted. "We've been following it! Stanley . . . ? Are you in there?"

"Yes!" Stanley called back. "I'm fine. The bank robbers are caught! They weren't ladies at all, just dressed that way!"

The handcuffed robbers were dreadfully **confuse**d. "Who's **yell**ing in our van? . . . Who stuck a balloon in the door? . . . Have we gone crazy?" they asked.

"It's my son Stanley," said Mr. Lambchop. "He is invisible, **unfortunately. Thank goodness** he was not hurt!"

"That must be the same invisible boy they had on TV!" said the first policeman.

"An invisible boy?" The tall robber **groan**ed. "After all my careful planning!"

The stout robber **shrug**ged. "You can't think of *everything*, Howard. Don't **blame** yourself."

The robbers were driven off to **jail**, and
Stanley went home with Mr. Lambchop in
a **cab**.

Stanley had been far too brave, Mrs.
Lambchop said when she heard what he
had done. Really! Flipping those ice cream
lids! Arthur said he'd have flipped them
too, if he'd thought of it.

Arthur's Storm

Mr. and Mrs. Lambchop had said good night. For a moment the brothers lay silent in their beds.

Then Arthur **yawn**ed. "Good night, Stanley. **Pleasant** dreams."

"Pleasant dreams? Hah!"

"Hah?"

"Those robbers today, they had *guns!*"

said Stanley. "They could have **shot** me **by accident** and nobody would even know."

"I never thought of that." Arthur sat up. "Are you mad at me?"

"I guess not. But . . ." Stanley **sigh**ed. "The thing is, I don't want to **go on** being in**visible**. I was really **scare**d today, and I hate carrying that balloon, but when I don't, people **bump** into me. And I can't see myself in the mirror, so I don't even remember how I look! It's like when I was flat. It was all right for a while, but then people **laugh**ed **at** me."

"That's why I blew you round again," Arthur said proudly. "Everyone said how smart I was."

"If you're so smart, get me out of *this*

fix!" There was a little **tremble** in Stanley's voice.

Arthur went to sit on the **edge** of his brother's bed. Feeling for a foot **beneath** the **cover**s, he **pat**ted it. "I'm really sorry for you," he said. "I wish—"

There was a **knock** at the door, and Mr. and Mrs. Lambchop came in. "Talking, you two? You ought to be asleep," they said.

Arthur explained about Stanley's unhappiness.

"There's more," Stanley said. "Twice my friends had parties and didn't invite me. They sometimes forget me even if I *do* keep **waving** that balloon!"

"Poor **dear**!" Mrs. Lambchop said. "'Out

of **sight**, out of mind,' as the **saying** goes."
She went to put her arms around Stanley,
but he had just sat up in bed and she
missed him. She found him and gave him
a hug.

"This is **awful**!" Arthur said. "We have
to *do* something!"

Mr. Lambchop shook his head. "Dr.
Dan knew of no **cure** for Stanley's
condition. And little about its cause **except**
for a possible **connection** between bad
weather and fruit."

"Then I'll always be like this." Stanley's
voice trembled again. "I'll get older and
bigger, but no one will ever see."

Arthur was thinking. "Stanley did eat
fruit. And there *was* a storm. Maybe . . .

Wait!"

He explained his idea.

Mr. and Mrs. Lambchop looked at each other, then at where they supposed Stanley to be, and at each other again.

"I'm not afraid," said Stanley. "Let's *try!*"

Mr. Lambchop **nod**ded. "I see no **harm** in it."

"Nor I," said Mrs. Lambchop. "Very well, Arthur! Let us **gather** what your plan **require**s!"

"Everyone ready?" said Arthur. "It has to be just the way it was the night Stanley got invisible."

"I'm wearing the same blue-and-white **stripe**y **pajamas**," said Stanley. "And I have an apple. And a box of raisins."

"We can't make a real storm," Arthur said. "But maybe this will work."

He stepped into the bathroom and **ran** the water in the **sink** and shower. "There's rain," he said, returning. "I'll be wind."

Mrs. Lambchop held up a **wooden** spoon and a large **skillet** from the kitchen. "**Thunder** ready," she said.

Mr. Lambchop showed the powerful **flashlight** he had **fetch**ed from his **tool kit**. "**Lightning** ready."

Stanley raised his apple. "Now?"

"Go stand by the window," said Arthur. "Now let me think. Hmmm . . . It was dark." He **put out** the light. "Go on, eat. *Whooosh!*" he added, being wind.

Stanley began to eat the apple.

Water **patter**ed down in the bathroom into the sink, and from the shower into the **tub**.

"*Whooosh . . . whooosh!*" said Arthur, and Mrs. Lambchop **struck** her skillet with the wooden spoon. The *crash!* was much like thunder.

"Lightning, please," Arthur said.

Mr. Lambchop **aim**ed his flashlight and **flick**ed it on and off while Stanley finished the apple.

"Now the raisins," said Arthur. "One at a time. *Whoooosh!*"

Stanley opened the little box and ate a raisin.

Still *whooosh*ing, Arthur **conduct**ed as if an **orchestra** sat before him. His left

hand **signal**ed Mrs. Lambchop to strike the skillet, the right one Mr. Lambchop to **flash** the light. Nods told Stanley when to eat a raisin.

Patter . . . splash went the water in the bathroom. *"Whooosh!"* went Arthur. *Crash!* went the skillet. *Flash! . . . Flash!* went the light.

"If anyone should see us now," Mrs. Lambchop said softly, "I would **be hard put to** explain."

Stanley looked down at himself. "It's no use," he said. "I'm still invisible."

"**Twist** around!" said Arthur. "Maybe the noise and light have to hit you just a certain way!"

Twisting, Stanley ate three more raisins.

The light **flicker**ed over him. He heard the water splashing, Arthur *whooosh*ing, the **pound**ing of the skillet with the spoon. How hard they were trying, he thought. How much he loved them all!

But he was still invisible.

"There's only one raisin left," he said. "It's no use."

"Poor Stanley!" cried Mrs. Lambchop.

Arthur could not **bear** the thought of never seeing his brother again. "Do the last raisin, Stanley," he said. "Do it!"

Stanley ate the raisin and did one more twist. Mrs. Lambchop **tap**ped her skillet and Mr. Lambchop flashed his light. Arthur gave a last *Whooosh!*

Nothing happened.

"At least I'm not hungry," Stanley said bravely. "But—" He put a hand to his **cheek**. "I feel . . . sort of **tingly**."

"Stanley!" said Mr. Lambchop. "Are you touching your cheek? I see your hand, I think!"

"And your pajamas!" shouted Arthur, **switch**ing **on** the light.

A sort of **outline** of Stanley Lambchop, with **hazy** stripes running up and down it, had appeared by the window. Through the stripes they could see the house **next door**.

Suddenly the outline **fill**ed in. There stood Stanley in his striped pajamas, just as they remembered him!

"I can see my feet!" Stanley shouted.

"It's *me!*"

"*I*, dear, not me," said Mrs. Lambchop before she could **catch herself**, then ran to hold him tight.

Mr. Lambchop shook hands with Arthur, and then they all went into the bathroom to watch Stanley look at himself in the mirror. It hadn't mattered when he was invisible, Mrs. Lambchop said, but he was greatly in need of a haircut now.

She made hot chocolate to **celebrate** the **occasion**, and Arthur's **clever**ness was **acknowledge**d by all.

"But false storms cannot be **relied** upon," Mr. Lambchop said. "We must **think twice** before eating fruit during bad weather. Especially by a window."

Then the brothers were **tuck**ed into bed again. "Good night," said Mr. and Mrs. Lambchop, putting out the light.

"Good night," said Stanley and Arthur.

Stanley got up and went to have another look in the bathroom mirror. "Thank you, Arthur," he said, coming back. "You saved me from being flat, and now you've saved me again."

"Oh, well . . ." Arthur yawned. "Stanley? Try to stay, you know, *regular* for a while."

"I will," said Stanley.

Soon they were both asleep.

The End

투명인간 스탠리

CONTENTS

미국 초등학생 사이에서 저스틴 비버보다 더 유명한 소년, 플랫 스탠리!

『플랫 스탠리(Flat Stanley)』 시리즈는 미국의 작가 제프 브라운(Jeff Brown)이 쓴 책으로, 한밤중에 몸 위로 떨어진 거대한 게시판에 눌려 납작해진(flat) 스탠리가 겪는 다양한 모험을 담고 있습니다. 플랫 스탠리는 아동 도서이지만 부모님들과 선생님들에게도 큰 사랑을 받으며, 출간된 지 50년이 넘은 지금까지 여러 세대를 아우르며 독자들에게 재미를 주고 있습니다. 미국에서만 100만 부 이상 판매된 『플랫 스탠리』 시리즈는 기존 챕터북 시리즈와 함께 플랫 스탠리의 세계 모험(Flat Stanley's Worldwide Adventures) 시리즈, 리더스북 등 다양한 형태로 출판되었고, 여러 언어로 번역되어 전 세계 독자들의 마음을 사로잡았습니다. 주인공 스탠리가 그려진 종이 인형을 만들어 이를 우편으로 원하는 사람에게 보내는 플랫 스탠리 프로젝트(The Flat Stanley Project)가 1995년에 시작된 이후, 이 책은 더 많은 관심을 받게 되었습니다. 유명 연예인은 물론 오바마 대통령까지 이 종이 인형과 함께 사진을 찍어 공유하는 등, 수많은 사례를 통해 시리즈의 높은 인기를 짐작할 수 있습니다.

이러한 『플랫 스탠리』 시리즈는 한국에서도 널리 알려져 '엄마표·아빠표 영어'를 진행하는 부모님과 초보 영어 학습자라면 반드시 읽어야 하는 영어원서로 자리 잡았습니다. 렉사일 지수가 최대 640L인 플랫 스탠리는 간결하지만 필수적인 어휘로 쓰여, 영어원서가 친숙하지 않은 학습자들에게도 즐거운 원서 읽기 경험을 선사할 것입니다.

번역과 단어장이 포함된 워크북, 그리고 오디오북까지 담긴 풀 패키지!

이 책은 영어원서 『플랫 스탠리』 시리즈에, 탁월한 학습 효과를 거둘 수 있도록 다양한 콘텐츠를 덧붙인 책입니다.

- 영어원서: 본문에 나온 어려운 어휘에 볼드 처리가 되어 있어 단어를 더욱 분명하게 인지할 수 있고, 문맥에 따른 자연스러운 암기 효과를 얻을 수 있습니다.
- 단어장: 원서에 볼드 처리된 어휘의 의미가 완벽하게 정리되어 있어 사전 없이 원서를 수월하게 읽을 수 있으며, 반복해서 등장하는 단어에 '복습' 표기를 하여 자연스럽게 복습을 돕도록 구성했습니다.

- 번역: 영문과 비교할 수 있도록 직역에 가까운 번역을 담았습니다. 원서 읽기에 익숙하지 않은 초보 학습자도 어려움 없이 내용을 파악할 수 있습니다.
- 퀴즈: 챕터별로 내용을 확인하는 이해력 점검 퀴즈가 들어 있습니다.
- 오디오북: 미국 현지에서 판매 중인 빠른 속도의 오디오북(분당 약 145단어)과 국내에서 녹음된 따라 읽기용 오디오북(분당 약 110단어)을 기본으로 포함하고 있어, 듣기 훈련은 물론 소리 내어 읽기에까지 폭넓게 활용할 수 있습니다.

이 책의 수준과 타깃 독자
- 미국 원어민 기준: 유치원 ~ 초등학교 저학년
- 한국 학습자 기준: 초등학교 저학년 ~ 중학생
- 영어원서 완독 경험이 없는 초보 영어 학습자
- 도서 분량: 약 5,900단어
- 비슷한 수준의 다른 챕터북: Arthur Chapter Book,★ The Zack Files,★ Tales from the Odyssey,★ Junie B. Jones,★ Magic Tree House, Marvin Redpost

  ★ 「롱테일 에디션」으로 출간된 도서

『플랫 스탠리』 이렇게 읽어 보세요!

- **단어 암기는 이렇게!** 처음 리딩을 시작하기 전, 오늘 읽을 챕터에 나오는 단어들을 눈으로 쭉 훑어봅니다. 모르는 단어는 좀 더 주의 깊게 보되, 손으로 쓰면서 완벽하게 암기할 필요는 없습니다. 본문을 읽으면서 이 단어를 다시 만나게 되는데, 그 과정에서 단어의 쓰임새와 어감을 자연스럽게 익히게 됩니다. 이렇게 책을 읽은 후에 단어를 다시 한번 복습하세요. 복습할 때는 중요하다고 생각하는 단어들을 손으로 쓰면서 꼼꼼하게 외우는 것도 좋습니다. 이런 방식으로 책을 읽으면 많은 단어를 빠르고 부담 없이 익힐 수 있습니다.

- **리딩할 때는 리딩에만 집중하자!** 원서를 읽는 중간중간 모르는 단어가 나온다고 워크북을 바로 펼쳐 보거나, 곧바로 번역을 찾아보는 것은 크게 도움이 되지 않습니다. 모르는 단어나 이해되지 않는 문장들은 따로 가볍게 표시만 해 두고, 전체적인 맥락을 파악하며 속도감 있게 읽어 나가세요. 리딩을 할 때는 속

도에 대한 긴장감을 잃지 않으면서 리딩에만 집중하는 것이 좋습니다. 모르는 단어와 문장은 리딩을 마친 후에 한꺼번에 정리하는 '리뷰' 시간을 통해 점검하는 시간을 가지면 됩니다. 리뷰를 할 때는 번역은 물론 단어장과 사전도 꼼꼼하게 확인하면서 어떤 이유에서 이해가 되지 않았는지 생각해 봅니다.

- **번역 활용은 이렇게!** 이해가 가지 않는 문장은 번역을 통해서 그 의미를 파악할 수 있습니다. 하지만 한국어와 영어는 정확히 1:1 대응이 되지 않기 때문에 번역을 활용하는 데에도 지혜가 필요합니다. 의역이 된 부분까지 억지로 의미를 대응해서 이해하려고 하기보다, 어떻게 그런 의미가 만들어진 것인지 추측하면서 번역은 참고 자료로 활용하는 것이 좋습니다.

- **듣기 훈련은 이렇게!** 리스닝 실력을 향상시키고 싶다면 오디오북을 적극적으로 활용해 보세요. 처음에는 오디오북을 틀어 놓고 눈으로 해당 내용을 따라 읽으면서 훈련을 하고, 이것이 익숙해지면 오디오북만 틀어 놓고 '귀를 통해' 책을 읽어 보세요. 눈으로 읽지 않은 책이라도 귀를 통해 이해할 수 있을 정도가 되면, 이후에 영어 듣기로 어려움을 겪는 일은 거의 없을 것입니다.

- **소리 내어 읽고 녹음하자!** 이 책은 특히 소리 내어 읽기(voice reading)에 최적화된 문장 길이와 구조를 가지고 있습니다. 오디오북 기본 구성에 포함된 '따라 읽기용' 오디오북을 활용해 소리 내어 읽기 훈련을 시작해 보세요! 내가 읽은 것을 녹음하고 들어보는 과정을 통해 자연스럽게 어휘와 표현을 복습하고, 의식적·무의식적으로 발음을 교정하게 됩니다. 이렇게 영어로 소리를 만들어 본 경험은 이후 탄탄한 스피킹 실력의 밑거름이 될 것입니다.

- **2~3번 반복해서 읽자!** 영어 초보자라면 처음부터 완벽하게 이해하려고 하는 것보다는 2~3회 반복해서 읽을 것을 추천합니다. 처음 원서를 읽을 때는 생소한 단어들과 스토리 때문에 내용 파악에 급급할 수밖에 없습니다. 하지만 일단 내용을 파악한 후에 다시 읽으면 문장 구조나 어휘의 활용에 더 집중하게 되고, 원서를 더 깊이 있게 읽을 수 있습니다. 그 과정에서 리딩 속도에 탄력이 붙고 리딩 실력 또한 더 확고히 다지게 됩니다.

● **'시리즈'로 꾸준히 읽자!** 한 작가의 책을 시리즈로 읽는 것 또한 영어 실력 향상에 큰 도움이 됩니다. 같은 등장인물이 다시 나오기 때문에 내용 파악이 더 수월할 뿐 아니라, 작가가 사용하는 어휘와 표현들도 반복되기 때문에 탁월한 복습 효과까지 얻을 수 있습니다. 롱테일북스의『플랫 스탠리』시리즈는 현재 6권, 총 35,700단어 분량이 출간되어 있습니다. 시리즈를 꾸준히 읽다 보면 영어 실력이 자연스럽게 향상될 것입니다.

원서 본문 구성

<u>내용이 담긴 원서 본문입니다.</u>
원어민이 읽는 일반 원서와 같은 텍스트지만, 암기해야 할 중요 어휘들은 볼드체로 표시되어 있습니다. 이 어휘들은 지금 들고 계신 워크북에 챕터별로 정리되어 있습니다.

학습 심리학 연구 결과에 따르면, 한 단어씩 따로 외우는 단어 암기는 거의 효과가 없다고 합니다. 단어를 제대로 외우기 위해서는 문맥(context) 속에서 단어를 암기해야 하며, 한 단어당 문맥 속에서 15번 이상 마주칠 때 완벽하게 암기할 수 있다고 합니다.
이 책의 본문에서는 중요 어휘를 볼드체로 강조하여, 문맥 속의 단어들을 더 확실히 인지(word cognition in context)하도록 돕고 있습니다. 또한 대부분의 중요 단어들은 다른 챕터에서도 반복해서 등장하기 때문에 이 책을 읽는 것만으로도 자연스럽게 어휘력을 향상시킬 수 있습니다.

본문 하단에는 내용 이해를 돕기 위한 '각주'가 첨가 되어 있습니다. 각주는 굳이 암기할 필요는 없지만, 알아 두면 도움이 될 만한 정보를 설명하고 있습니다. 각주를 참고하면 스토리를 더 깊이 있게 이해할 수 있어 원서를 읽는 재미가 배가됩니다.

워크북(Workbook) 구성

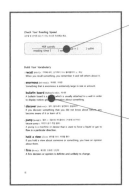

Check Your Reading Speed
해당 챕터의 단어 수가 기록되어 있어, 리딩 속도를 측정할 수 있습니다. 특히 리딩 속도를 중시하는 독자들이 유용하게 사용할 수 있습니다.

Build Your Vocabulary
본문에 볼드 표시되어 있는 단어들이 정리되어 있습니다. 리딩 전·후에 반복해서 보면 원서를 더욱 쉽게 읽을 수 있고, 어휘력도 빠르게 향상될 것입니다.

단어는 〈스펠링 – 빈도 – 발음기호 – 품사 – 한글 뜻 – 영문 뜻〉 순서로 표기되어 있으며 빈도 표시(★)가 많을수록 필수 어휘입니다. 반복해서 등장하는 단어는 빈도 대신 '복습'으로 표기되어 있습니다. 품사는 아래와 같이 표기했습니다.

n. 명사 │ a. 형용사 │ ad. 부사 │ v. 동사
conj. 접속사 │ prep. 전치사 │ int. 감탄사 │ idiom 숙어 및 관용구

Comprehension Quiz
간단한 퀴즈를 통해 읽은 내용에 대한 이해력을 점검해 볼 수 있습니다.

한국어 번역
영문과 비교할 수 있도록 최대한 직역에 가까운 번역을 담았습니다.

오디오북 구성

이 책에는 '듣기 훈련'과 '소리 내어 읽기 훈련'을 위한 2가지 종류의 오디오북이
기본으로 포함되어 있습니다.

- 듣기 훈련용 오디오북: 분당 145단어 속도 (미국 현지에서 판매 중인 오디오북)
- 따라 읽기용 오디오북: 분당 110단어 속도 (소리 내어 읽기 훈련용 오디오북)

 QR코드를 인식하여 따라 읽기용 & 듣기 훈련용 두 가지 오디오북을 들어
보세요! 더불어 롱테일북스 홈페이지 (www.longtailbooks.co.kr)에서도
오디오북 MP3 파일을 다운로드 받을 수 있습니다.

Prologue

1. Why couldn't Stanley sleep?

    A. The rain was keeping him awake.

    B. The bedroom was too dark and scary.

    C. He was worried about Arthur.

    D. He had just eaten a big meal.

2. What made Arthur wake up?

    A. The sound of the rain

    B. The sound of thunder

    C. The sound of Stanley's voice

    D. The sound of Stanley's stomach

3. **What happened as Stanley ate the apple?**

    A. The rain outside got lighter.

    B. The rain outside got heavier.

    C. Stanley became sleepy.

    D. Stanley became full.

4. **Where did Stanley get raisins from?**

    A. He got them from under Arthur's bed.

    B. He got them from a shelf by the window.

    C. He got them from a bowl in the kitchen.

    D. He got them from a desk drawer.

5. **What happened after Stanley ate the raisins?**

    A. He still felt hungry.

    B. He felt satisfied.

    C. He felt a little sick.

    D. He felt a bit strange.

Check Your Reading Speed

1분에 몇 단어를 읽는지 리딩 속도를 측정해보세요.

$$\frac{143 \text{ words}}{\text{reading time ( ) sec}} \times 60 = (\quad) \text{ WPM}$$

Build Your Vocabulary

☆ **respond** [rispánd] v. 대답하다, 응답하다; 반응을 보이다 (response n. 대답; 반응)
Your response to an event or to something that is said is your reply or reaction to it.

☆ **fetch** [feʧ] v. 가지고 오다, 데리고 오다; (특정 가격에) 팔리다; n. 가져옴, 데려옴
If you fetch something or someone, you go and get them from the place where they are.

worsen [wɔːrsn] v. 악화되다
If a bad situation worsens or if something worsens it, it becomes more difficult, unpleasant, or unacceptable.

☆ **shelf** [ʃelf] n. 선반; (책장의) 칸
A shelf is a flat piece of wood, metal, or glass which is attached to a wall or to the sides of a cupboard.

★ **murmur** [mɔ́ːrmər] v. 속삭이다, 소곤거리다, 중얼거리다; n. 속삭임, 소곤거림
If you murmur something, you say it very quietly, so that not many people can hear what you are saying.

☆ **crash** [kræʃ] n. 요란한 소리; (자동차·항공기) 사고; v. 충돌하다; 박살나다; 쾅음을 내다
A crash is a sudden, loud noise.

★ **thunder** [θʌ́ndər] n. 천둥; v. 천둥이 치다; 우르릉거리다
Thunder is the loud noise that you hear from the sky after a flash of lightning, especially during a storm.

* **lightning** [láitniŋ] n. 번개, 번갯불; a. 아주 빨리; 급작스럽게

Lightning is the very bright flashes of light in the sky that happen during thunderstorms.

* **flash** [flæʃ] v. (잠깐) 번쩍이다; (눈 등이) 번득이다; 휙 움직이다; n. 번쩍임; 순간

If a light flashes or if you flash a light, it shines with a sudden bright light, especially as quick, regular flashes of light.

* **yawn** [jɔːn] v. 하품하다; n. 하품

If you yawn, you open your mouth very wide and breathe in more air than usual, often when you are tired or when you are not interested in something.

Where Is Stanley?

1. What did Arthur tell Mr. and Mrs. Lambchop?

A. He told them that Stanley had run away.

B. He told them that Stanley might be hurt.

C. He told them that he couldn't find Stanley.

D. He told them that he couldn't hear Stanley.

2. What did Mr. and Mrs. Lambchop see in the bedroom?

A. They saw Stanley's head resting on his pillow.

B. They saw the shape of a body beneath Stanley's covers.

C. They saw pillows stuffed under Stanley's covers.

D. They saw Stanley wearing slippers on his bed.

3. **What happened when Stanley put on clothes?**

   A. The clothes became invisible.

   B. The clothes changed colors.

   C. Stanley reappeared.

   D. Stanley became smaller.

4. **Why did Arthur give Stanley a balloon?**

   A. He thought it would make Stanley feel better.

   B. He thought it would transform Stanley back into a normal boy.

   C. He thought it would make his parents laugh.

   D. He thought it would help the family keep track of Stanley.

5. **What happened when Stanley held the string tied to the balloon?**

   A. Only the balloon disappeared.

   B. Only the string disappeared.

   C. Both the balloon and the string disappeared.

   D. Neither the balloon nor the string disappeared.

Check Your Reading Speed

1분에 몇 단어를 읽는지 리딩 속도를 측정해보세요.

$$\frac{469 \text{ words}}{\text{reading time ( ) sec}} \times 60 = (\qquad) \text{ WPM}$$

Build Your Vocabulary

★ **recall** [rikɔ́ːl] v. 기억해 내다, 상기하다; 다시 불러들이다; n. 회상
When you recall something, you remember it and tell others about it.

★ **enormous** [inɔ́ːrməs] a. 막대한, 거대한
Something that is enormous is extremely large in size or amount.

bulletin board [búlitən bɔːrd] n. 게시판
A bulletin board is a board which is usually attached to a wall in order to display notices giving information about something.

‡ **discover** [diskʌ́vər] v. 찾다, 알아내다; 발견하다; 발굴하다
If you discover something that you did not know about before, you become aware of it or learn of it.

★ **pump** [pʌmp] n. 펌프; v. (펌프로) 퍼 올리다; (거세게) 솟구치다
(bicycle pump n. 자전거 공기 주입 펌프)
A pump is a machine or device that is used to force a liquid or gas to flow in a particular direction.

hold a view idiom 생각을 갖다, 의견을 품다
If you hold a view about someone or something, you have an opinion about them.

‡ **firm** [fəːrm] a. 확고한, 단호한; 단단한
A firm decision or opinion is definite and unlikely to change.

‌* **hay** [hei] n. 건초
Hay is grass which has been cut and dried so that it can be used to feed animals.

* **visible** [vízəbl] a. (눈에) 보이는, 알아볼 수 있는; 뚜렷한 (invisible a. 보이지 않는)
If something is visible, it can be seen.

⁎ **beneath** [biníːθ] prep. 아래에; ~보다 못한
Something that is beneath another thing is under the other thing.

⁎⁎ **cover** [kávər] n. 덮개, 커버; 몸을 숨길 곳; v. (감추거나 보호하기 위해) 씌우다; 덮다
The covers on your bed are the things such as sheets and blankets that you have on top of you.

* **pillow** [pílou] n. 베개
A pillow is a rectangular cushion which you rest your head on when you are in bed.

* **squash** [skwaʃ] v. 짓누르다, 으깨다; (좁은 곳에) 밀어 넣다
If someone or something is squashed, they are pressed or crushed with such force that they become injured or lose their shape.

⁎⁎ **rest** [rest] v. 놓이다, (~에) 있다; 쉬다; n. 나머지; 휴식
If something is resting somewhere, or if you are resting it there, it is in a position where its weight is supported.

* **stare** [stɛər] v. 빤히 쳐다보다, 응시하다; n. 빤히 쳐다보기, 응시
If you stare at someone or something, you look at them for a long time.

⁎ **pair** [pɛər] n. 한 쌍; 두 사람; v. (둘씩) 짝을 짓다
A pair of things are two things of the same size and shape that are used together or are both part of something, for example shoes, earrings, or parts of the body.

* **slipper** [slípər] n. 슬리퍼, 실내화
Slippers are loose, soft shoes that you wear at home.

* **explore** [iksplɔ́:r] v. (손이나 발로) 더듬어 보다; 탐험하다, 탐사하다
If you explore something with your hands or fingers, you touch it to find out what it feels like.

* **ouch** [auʧ] int. 아야 (갑자기 아파서 내지르는 소리)
'Ouch!' is used in writing to represent the noise that people make when they suddenly feel pain.

* **poke** [pouk] v. (손가락 등으로) 쿡 찌르다; 쑥 내밀다; n. (손가락 등으로) 찌르기
If you poke someone or something, you quickly push them with your finger or with a sharp object.

* **gasp** [gæsp] v. 숨이 턱 막히다, 헉 하고 숨을 쉬다; n. 헉 하는 소리를 냄
When you gasp, you take a short quick breath through your mouth, especially when you are surprised, shocked, or in pain.

* **giggle** [gigl] n. 피식 웃음, 킥킥거림; v. 피식 웃다, 킥킥거리다
A giggle is a high laugh, especially a nervous or silly one.

* **tickle** [tikl] v. 간질간질하다; 간지럽히다; n. (장난으로) 간지럽히기
If something tickles you or tickles, it causes an irritating feeling by lightly touching a part of your body.

* **accidental** [æksədéntl] a. 우연한, 돌발적인 (accidentally ad. 우연히, 뜻하지 않게)
An accidental event happens by chance or as the result of an accident, and is not deliberately intended.

* **summon** [sʌ́mən] v. 호출하다, (오라고) 부르다; 소환하다
If you summon someone, you order them to come to you.

draw a breath idiom 깊이 숨쉬다, 심호흡하다
If you draw a deep breath, you breathe in deeply once.

‡ **face** [feis] v. (힘든 사실을) 받아들이다; 직면하다; n. 얼굴
If you face the truth or face the facts, you accept that something is true.

startle [stɑ́:rtl] v. 깜짝 놀라게 하다; n. 깜짝 놀람 (startled a. 놀란)
If something sudden and unexpected startles you, it surprises and frightens you slightly.

pajamas [pədʒɑ́:məz] n. (바지와 상의로 된) 잠옷
A pair of pajamas consists of loose trousers and a loose jacket that people, especially men, wear in bed.

vanish [vǽniʃ] v. 사라지다, 없어지다; 모습을 감추다
If someone or something vanishes, they disappear suddenly or in a way that cannot be explained.

reappear [rì:əpíər] v. 다시 나타나다
When people or things reappear, they return again after they have been away or out of sight for some time.

trouser [tráuzər] n. (pl.) 바지; 바지의 한쪽
Trousers are a piece of clothing that you wear over your body from the waist downward, and that cover each leg separately.

gracious [gréiʃəs] int. 세상에!, 맙소사!; a. 자애로운, 품위 있는; 우아한
Some people say 'gracious' or 'goodness gracious' in order to express surprise or annoyance.

track [træk] n. 자국; 선로; 방향, 진로; v. 추적하다; 발자국을 남기다
(keep track of idiom ~에 대해 계속 알고 있다)
If you keep track of a situation or a person, you make sure that you have the newest and most accurate information about them all the time.

dear [diər] n. 얘야; 여보, 당신; int. 이런!, 맙소사!; a. 사랑하는; ~에게
You can call someone dear as a sign of affection.

tie [tai] v. (끈 등으로) 묶다; 결부시키다; n. 끈; 유대 (untie v. (매듭 등을) 풀다)
If you untie something that is tied to another thing, you remove the string or rope that holds them or that has been tied round them.

party favor [pá:rti feivər] n. (손님에게 주는 작은) 파티 선물
A party favor is a small gift that people give to children at a party.

‡ **float** [flout] v. (물 위나 공중에서) 떠가다; (물에) 뜨다; n. 부표
Something that floats in or through the air hangs in it or moves slowly and gently through it.

‡ **string** [striŋ] n. 끈, 줄; 일련; v. 묶다, 매달다; (실 등에) 꿰다
String is thin rope made of twisted threads, used for tying things together or tying up parcels.

⁎ **approximate** [əprɑ́ksəmət] a. 비슷한, 근사한 (approximately ad. 거의 (정확하게))
An approximate number, time, or position is close to the correct number, time, or position, but is not exact.

make of idiom ~라고 이해하다, ~라고 생각하다
To make of someone or something means to understand someone or the meaning of something in a particular way.

Dr. Dan

1. How did Dr. Dan react when invisible Stanley first spoke?

A. He acted like Stanley's condition was very serious.

B. He wasn't surprised that something strange had happened to Stanley again.

C. He seemed uncomfortable talking to someone that he couldn't see.

D. He assumed Mr. Lambchop was playing a trick on him.

2. What symptom did Stanley have?

A. He didn't have any symptoms.

B. He just had a headache.

C. He had a sore throat and an upset stomach.

D. His whole body ached.

3. What did Dr. Dan think caused Stanley's condition?

A. Reading too many books about disappearances

B. Eating too much fruit at a young age

C. Staying up late during bad weather

D. Eating fruit during bad weather

4. Why did Dr. Dan suggest that the Lambchops go to a textile specialist?

A. To have new clothes made for Stanley

B. To ask why Stanley's clothes vanish

C. To find out why Stanley had become invisible

D. To check Stanley's health

5. Why did Mrs. Lambchop replace the red balloon with a different one?

A. She wanted to get rid of the red balloon because it was old.

B. She wanted to paint a silly face on another balloon to cheer everyone up.

C. She wanted to decorate another balloon to look more like Stanley.

D. She wanted to practice her painting skills on another balloon.

Check Your Reading Speed

1분에 몇 단어를 읽는지 리딩 속도를 측정해보세요.

$$\frac{467\ words}{reading\ time\ (\quad)\ sec} \times 60 = (\quad)\ WPM$$

Build Your Vocabulary

never mind idiom 신경쓰지 마
You use never mind to tell someone that they need not do something or worry about something, because it is not important or because you will do it yourself.

＊ **fellow** [félou] n. 녀석, 친구; 동료; a. 동료의
A fellow is a man or boy.

see through idiom ~을 간파하다, 꿰뚫어 보다
If you see through something, you recognize that it is not true and not be tricked by it.

＊ **joke** [dʒouk] n. 농담; 웃음거리; v. 농담하다; 농담삼아 말하다
A joke is something that is said or done to make you laugh, for example a funny story.

＊ **beg** [beg] v. 간청하다, 애원하다; 구걸하다
If you beg someone to do something, you ask them very anxiously or eagerly to do it.

＊ **pardon** [paːrdn] int. 뭐라고요; n. 용서; v. 용서하다 (beg pardon idiom 뭐라고요)
You say 'I beg your pardon?' when you want someone to repeat what they have just said because you have not heard or understood it.

복습 **visible** [vízəbl] a. (눈에) 보이는, 알아볼 수 있는; 뚜렷한 (invisible a. 보이지 않는)
If you describe something as invisible, you mean that it cannot be seen, for example because it is transparent, hidden, or very small.

24

unsettle [ʌ̀nsétl] v. (사람을) 불안하게 하다, 동요시키다 (unsettled a. 불안해하는)
If you are unsettled, you cannot concentrate on anything because you are worried.

⋆ **headache** [hédeik] n. 두통
If you have a headache, you have a pain in your head.

⁑ **throat** [θrout] n. 목구멍, 목
Your throat is the back of your mouth and the top part of the tubes that go down into your stomach and your lungs.

⁑ **sore** [sɔːr] a. 아픈, 화끈거리는; 화가 난, 감정이 상한
If part of your body is sore, it causes you pain and discomfort.

⁑ **stomach** [stʌ́mək] n. 복부, 배
Your stomach is the organ inside your body where food is digested before it moves into the intestines.

⁑ **upset** [ʌpsét] a. 불편한; 속상한, 마음이 상한; v. 속상하게 하다 (stomach upset n. 배탈)
A stomach upset is a slight illness in your stomach caused by an infection or by something that you have eaten.

⋆ **frankly** [frǽŋkli] ad. 솔직히, 솔직히 말하면
You use frankly when you are expressing an opinion or feeling to emphasize that you mean what you are saying, especially when the person you are speaking to may not like it.

⁑ **despite** [dispáit] prep. ~에도 불구하고
You use despite to introduce a fact which makes the other part of the sentence surprising.

⁑ **practice** [prǽktis] n. (의사·변호사 등의) 업무; 실행; 연습; v. 연습하다
The work done by doctors and lawyers is referred to as the practice of medicine and law.

run into idiom (곤경 등을) 겪다; ~를 우연히 만나다
To run into something means to experience difficulties or problems.

‡ **medical** [médikəl] a. 의학의, 의료의
Medical means relating to illness and injuries and to their treatment or prevention.

* **peculiar** [pikjú:ljər] a. 이상한, 기이한; 고유한
If you describe someone or something as peculiar, you think that they are strange or unusual, sometimes in an unpleasant way.

‡ **case** [keis] n. (특정한 상황의) 경우; 사건; 용기, 통, 상자
A case is a person or their particular problem that a doctor, social worker, or other professional is dealing with.

복습 **shelf** [ʃelf] n. 선반; (책장의) 칸
A shelf is a flat piece of wood, metal, or glass which is attached to a wall or to the sides of a cupboard.

* **disappear** [dìsəpíər] v. 사라지다, 보이지 않게 되다; 없어지다
(disappearance n. 사라짐)
If you say that someone or something disappears, you mean that you can no longer see them, usually because you or they have changed position.

복습 **vanish** [vǽniʃ] v. 사라지다, 없어지다; 모습을 감추다
If someone or something vanishes, they disappear suddenly or in a way that cannot be explained.

복습 **lightning** [láitniŋ] n. 번개, 번갯불; a. 아주 빨리; 급작스럽게
Lightning is the very bright flashes of light in the sky that happen during thunderstorms.

‡ **observe** [əbzə́:rv] v. ~을 보다; 관찰하다; (발언·의견을) 말하다
If you observe someone or something, you see or notice them.

* **chief** [tʃi:f] n. (조직·집단의) 장(長); a. (계급·직급상) 최고위자인
The chief of a tribe is its leader.

* **canned** [kænd] a. 통조림으로 된
When food or drink is canned, it is put into a metal container and sealed so that it will remain fresh.

blizzard [blízzərd] n. 눈보라
A blizzard is a very bad snowstorm with strong winds.

suspect [səspékt] v. 의심하다; 수상쩍어 하다; n. 용의자
You use suspect when you are stating something that you believe is probably true, in order to make it sound less strong or direct.

connection [kənékʃən] n. 관련성; 연결, 접속
A connection is a relationship between two things, people, or groups.

storm [stɔːrm] v. 폭풍이 불다; 쿵쾅대며 가다; n. 폭풍
When it storms, the weather is violent, with strong winds and usually rain, thunder, lightning, or snow.

look on the bright side idiom 긍정적으로 보다
If you look on the bright side, you try to be cheerful about a bad situation by thinking of some advantages, or thinking that it is not as bad as it could have been.

except [iksépt] prep. 제외하고는
You use except for to introduce the only thing or person that prevents a statement from being completely true.

visibility [vìzəbíləti] n. 눈에 잘 보임, 가시성; 시계(視界)
If you refer to the visibility of something such as a situation or problem, you mean how much it is seen or noticed by other people.

factor [fǽktər] n. 요인, 요소
A factor is one of the things that affects an event, decision, or situation.

keep an eye on idiom ~을 계속 지켜보다
If you keep an eye on someone or something, you watch or check them to make sure that they are safe.

field [fiːld] n. 분야; 들판, 밭; 현장
A particular field is a particular subject of study or type of activity.

suggest [səgdʒést] v. 제안하다, 제의하다; 암시하다
If you suggest the name of a person or place, you recommend them to someone.

textile [tékstail] n. 직물, 옷감
Textiles are types of cloth or fabric, especially ones that have been woven.

specialist [spéʃəlist] n. 전문가
A specialist is a person who has a particular skill or knows a lot about a particular subject.

dear [diər] n. 얘야; 여보, 당신; int. 이런!, 맙소사!; a. 사랑하는; ~에게
You can call someone dear as a sign of affection.

locate [lóukeit] v. ~의 정확한 위치를 찾아내다; (특정 위치에) 두다
If you locate something or someone, you find out where they are.

remind [rimáind] v. 상기시키다, 다시 한 번 알려 주다
If someone reminds you of a fact or event that you already know about, they say something which makes you think about it.

artistic [ɑːrtístik] a. 예술적 감각이 있는; 예술의 (artistically ad. 예술적으로)
Someone who is artistic is good at drawing or painting, or arranging things in a beautiful way.

talented [tǽləntid] a. 재능이 있는
Someone who is talented has a natural ability to do something well.

replace [ripléis] v. 대신하다, 대체하다; 교체하다
If you replace one thing or person with another, you put something or someone else in their place to do their job.

delicate [délikət] a. 섬세한, 우아한; 연약한, 여린
A delicate task, movement, action, or product needs or shows great skill and attention to detail.

brush [brʌʃ] n. 붓질, 솔질; 붓; 솔; 비; v. ~을 스치다; 솔질을 하다
A brush is an act of sweeping, applying, or arranging with a brush or with one's hand.

likeness [láiknis] n. 초상(肖像), 화상; 유사성, 닮음
A likeness of someone is a picture or sculpture of them.

at once idiom 즉시; 동시에
If you do something at once, you do it immediately.

cheerful [ʧíərfəl] a. 발랄한, 쾌활한; 쾌적한
Someone who is cheerful is happy and shows this in their behavior.

The First Days

1. What did Miss Benchley say to the class about Stanley?

   A. She said the class should not gossip about Stanley.

   B. She said the class should not talk to Stanley.

   C. She said the class should be extra kind to Stanley.

   D. She said the class should pay more attention to Stanley.

2. Where did the "Before" photograph of Stanley come from?

   A. It was taken by Mrs. Lambchop at home.

   B. It was taken by a reporter in Stanley's classroom.

   C. It was taken by one of Stanley's classmates at his desk.

   D. It was taken by Miss Benchley at school.

3. What did Arthur think about the story in the paper?
   A. He thought the "Before" and "After" pictures looked nice.
   B. He thought the photograph of the balloon did not look good.
   C. He thought it would have been better with a picture of him.
   D. He thought it would have been more interesting with a different headline.

4. What is one temptation that Mr. and Mrs. Lambchop want Stanley to avoid?
   A. Sneaking up on people and then scaring them
   B. Listening secretly to other people's conversations
   C. Lying to people about his location
   D. Going to places alone without permission

5. What happened at the movie theater?
   A. Stanley moved to another seat.
   B. Stanley stayed in his seat during the whole movie.
   C. Stanley blocked other people's view.
   D. Stanley sat on Mrs. Lambchop's lap.

Check Your Reading Speed

1분에 몇 단어를 읽는지 리딩 속도를 측정해보세요.

$$\frac{424 \ words}{reading \ time \ (\quad) \ sec} \times 60 = (\quad) \ WPM$$

Build Your Vocabulary

^{복습} tie [tai] v. (끈 등으로) 묶다; 결부시키다; n. 끈; 유대
If you tie two things together or tie them, you fasten them together with a knot.

^{복습} string [striŋ] n. 끈, 줄; 일련; v. 묶다, 매달다; (실 등에) 꿰다
String is thin rope made of twisted threads, used for tying things together or tying up parcels.

＊ unexpected [ʌ̀nikspéktid] a. 예기치 않은, 예상 밖의
(unexpectedly ad. 뜻밖에, 예상외로)
If an event or someone's behavior is unexpected, it surprises you because you did not think that it was likely to happen.

＊ guide [gaid] n. 지침, 지표; 안내(서); (여행) 안내인; v. 안내하여 데려가다; 인도하다
A guide is something that can be used to help you plan your actions or to form an opinion about something.

＊ presence [prézns] n. (특정한 곳에) 있음, 존재(함), 참석
Someone's presence in a place is the fact that they are there.

＊ sincere [sinsíər] a. 진실된, 진심 어린; 진심의 (sincerely ad. ～올림)
People write 'Sincerely' before their signature at the end of a formal letter when they have addressed it to someone by name.

^{복습} stare [stɛər] v. 빤히 쳐다보다, 응시하다; n. 빤히 쳐다보기, 응시
If you stare at someone or something, you look at them for a long time.

* **gossip** [gásəp] v. 험담을 하다; n. 소문, 험담; 수다
If you gossip with someone, you talk informally, especially about other people or local events.

‡ **state** [steit] n. 상태; 국가; 주(州); v. 말하다, 진술하다
When you talk about the state of someone or something, you are referring to the condition they are in or what they are like at a particular time.

* **nevertheless** [nèvərðəlés] ad. 그럼에도 불구하고
You use nevertheless when saying something that contrasts with what has just been said.

‡ **reach** [ri:tʃ] v. ~에 이르다; (손·팔을) 뻗다; n. (닿을 수 있는) 거리; 범위
If something reaches someone, they receive it after it has been sent to them.

* **reporter** [ripɔ́:rtər] n. (보도) 기자, 리포터
A reporter is someone who writes news articles or who broadcasts news.

* **headline** [hédlain] n. (신문 기사의) 표제; v. (기사에) 표제를 달다
A headline is the title of a newspaper story, printed in large letters at the top of the story, especially on the front page.

복습 **beneath** [biní:θ] prep. 아래에; ~보다 못한
Something that is beneath another thing is under the other thing.

bob [bab] v. 위아래로 움직이다; (고개를) 까닥거리다; n. (머리·몸을) 까닥거림
If something bobs, it moves up and down, like something does when it is floating on water.

* **include** [inklú:d] v. 포함하다; ~을 (~에) 포함시키다
If one thing includes another thing, it has the other thing as one of its parts.

knowledge [nálidʒ] n. 알고 있음; 지식
(to the best of one's knowledge idiom ~가 알고 있는 바로는)
If you say that something is true to the best of your knowledge, you mean that you believe it to be true but it is possible that you do not know all the facts.

out-of-town [àut-əv-táun] a. 다른 곳에서 온
Out-of-town is used to describe people who do not live in a particular town or city, but have traveled there for a particular purpose.

artwork [á:rtwə:rk] n. 미술품; 도판, 삽화
Artworks are paintings or sculptures which are of high quality.

on the whole idiom 전체적으로 보아, 대체로
You use on the whole to indicate that what you are saying is true in general but may not be true in every case, or that you are giving a general opinion or summary of something.

suggest [səgdʒést] v. 제안하다, 제의하다; 암시하다
If you suggest something, you put forward a plan or idea for someone to think about.

tempt [tempt] v. 유혹하다; 유도하다 (temptation n. 유혹)
If you feel you want to do something or have something, even though you know you really should avoid it, you can refer to this feeling as temptation.

warn [wɔ:rn] v. 경고하다, 주의를 주다, 조심하라고 하다
If you warn someone about something such as a possible danger or problem, you tell them about it so that they are aware of it.

resist [rizíst] v. 참다, 견디다; 저항하다; 굴하지 않다
If you resist doing something, or resist the temptation to do it, you stop yourself from doing it although you would like to do it.

spy [spai] v. 염탐하다; (갑자기) 보다, 알아채다; n. 스파이, 정보원
If you spy on someone, you watch them secretly.

34

* **sneak** [sni:k] v. 살금살금 가다; 몰래 하다; a. 기습적인
(sneak up idiom 살금살금 다가가다)
If you sneak up on someone, you approach them very quietly, so that they do not see or hear you until you reach them.

* **whisper** [hwíspər] v. 속삭이다, 소곤거리다; n. 속삭임, 소곤거리는 소리
When you whisper, you say something very quietly, using your breath rather than your throat, so that only one person can hear you.

* **deceitful** [disí:tfəl] a. 남을 기만하는, 부정직한
If you say that someone is deceitful, you mean that they behave in a dishonest way by making other people believe something that is not true.

* **tuck** [tʌk] v. 집어 넣다, 끼워 넣다; 단단히 덮어 주다; n. 주름, 단
If you tuck something somewhere, you put it there so that it is safe, comfortable, or neat.

‡ **block** [blak] v. 막다, 차단하다; 방해하다; n. 구역, 블록; 사각형 덩어리
If something blocks your view, it prevents you from seeing something because it is between you and that thing.

* **lap** [læp] n. 무릎; (트랙의) 한 바퀴
If you have something on your lap when you are sitting down, it is on top of your legs and near to your body.

‡ **screen** [skri:n] n. (영화·텔레비전) 화면; 칸막이, 가리개; v. 가리다, 차단하다
A screen is a flat vertical surface on which pictures or words are shown.

go to sleep idiom (팔·다리가) 저리다
If your arms or legs go to sleep, you are unable to feel anything in them because they have been in a particular position for a long time.

In the Park

1. Why did Stanley decide to help Billy?

A. He thought that he could show Billy fun ways to ride a bike.

B. He was concerned that Billy would fall off his bike unless someone helped him.

C. He remembered how hard it had been when he was first learning to ride a bike.

D. He wanted to prove how fast he could run while pushing a bike.

2. How did Mr. Lambchop react to Billy winning?

A. He wondered how Billy was suddenly able to ride so well.

B. He was impressed by how talented Billy was at bike riding.

C. He felt very sorry that Stanley hadn't seen Billy win.

D. He pretended he didn't know that Stanley had helped Billy.

3. **What was the problem with Phillip?**

    A. He wasn't in love with Lucia.

    B. He didn't have the courage to ask Lucia to marry him.

    C. He wasn't sure if Lucia wanted to marry him.

    D. He had proposed to Lucia many times before, but she had always said no.

4. **How did Phillip react when Lucia agreed to marry him?**

    A. He was excited to share the news with everyone he knew.

    B. He was relieved that Lucia hadn't rejected him.

    C. He felt disappointed that he hadn't proposed on his own.

    D. He didn't realize that he hadn't really proposed.

5. **How did Mr. and Mrs. Lambchop feel about Stanley helping Phillip?**

    A. They thought that Stanley had done a good job.

    B. They were upset that Stanley had spied on others.

    C. They believed that Stanley should not have talked to Phillip.

    D. They were nervous that Mrs. Hodgson would find out what had happened.

Check Your Reading Speed

1분에 몇 단어를 읽는지 리딩 속도를 측정해보세요.

$$\frac{1,123 \text{ words}}{\text{reading time ( ) sec}} \times 60 = (\quad) \text{ WPM}$$

Build Your Vocabulary

set out idiom (여행을) 시작하다; ~을 진열하다
If you set out, you leave a place and begin a journey, especially a long journey.

⁚crowd [kraud] v. 가득 메우다; (생각이 마음속에) 밀려오다; n. 사람들, 군중
(crowded a. 붐비는)
If a place is crowded, it is full of people.

⁎lessen [lesn] v. 줄다, 작게 하다
If something lessens or you lessen it, it becomes smaller in size, amount, degree, or importance.

⁚risk [risk] n. 위험; v. 위태롭게 하다
If there is a risk of something unpleasant, there is a possibility that it will happen.

jostle [dʒasl] v. 거칠게 밀치다; n. 충돌
If people jostle you, they bump against you or push you in a way that annoys you, usually because you are in a crowd and they are trying to get past you.

⁚college [kálidʒ] n. 대학(교)
A college is an institution where students study for degrees and where academic research is done.

⁚treat [tri:t] n. 기쁨; (대접하는) 특별한 것; v. (특정한 태도로) 대하다; 치료하다; 대접하다
A treat is a special and enjoyable occasion or experience.

^복_습run into idiom ~를 우연히 만나다; (곤경 등을) 겪다

To run into someone means to meet them by chance.

^복_습recall [rikɔ́:l] v. 기억해 내다, 상기하다; 다시 불러들이다; n. 회상

When you recall something, you remember it and tell others about it.

^복roll [roul] v. (둥글게) 말다; 걷어 올리다; 구르다; n. 뒹굴기; 구르기

If you roll something, you fold it or wrap it around itself so that it forms a tube or a ball.

^복foreign [fɔ́:rən] a. 외국의; 대외의

Something or someone that is foreign comes from or relates to a country that is not your own.

_*lad [læd] n. 사내애; 청년

A lad is a young man or boy.

take care idiom 안녕, 잘 가; ~을 처리하다; ~을 돌보다

You can say 'take care' when saying goodbye to someone.

^복_습float [flout] v. (물 위나 공중에서) 떠가다; (물에) 뜨다; n. 부표

Something that floats in or through the air hangs in it or moves slowly and gently through it.

^복_습visible [vízəbl] a. (눈에) 보이는, 알아볼 수 있는; 뚜렷한 (invisible a. 보이지 않는)

If you describe something as invisible, you mean that it cannot be seen, for example because it is transparent, hidden, or very small.

_*dental [dentl] a. 치과의

Dental is used to describe things that relate to teeth or to the care and treatment of teeth.

remember to idiom ~에게 안부를 전하다

If you ask someone to remember you to a person who you have not seen for a long time, you are asking them to pass your greetings on to that person.

★ **remarkable** [rimá:rkəbl] a. 놀랄 만한, 놀라운; 주목할 만한
Someone or something that is remarkable is unusual or special in a way that makes people notice them and be surprised or impressed.

복습 **field** [fi:ld] n. 들판, 밭; 분야; 현장
A field is an area of grass, for example in a park or on a farm.

복습 **rest** [rest] v. 쉬다; 놓이다, (~에) 있다; n. 나머지; 휴식
If you rest or if you rest your body, you do not do anything active for a time.

race [reis] v. 경주하다; 쏜살같이 가다; n. 경주; 경쟁; 인종, 종족
If you race a vehicle or animal, you prepare it for races and make it take part in races.

give up idiom 포기하다; 그만두다; 단념하다
If you give up, you stop trying to do something, usually because it is too difficult.

‡ **silly** [síli] a. 어리석은, 바보 같은; 우스꽝스러운; n. 바보
If you say that someone or something is silly, you mean that they are foolish, childish, or ridiculous.

복습 **fellow** [félou] n. 녀석, 친구; 동료; a. 동료의
A fellow is a man or boy.

복습 **dear** [diər] int. 이런!, 맙소사!; n. 얘야; 여보, 당신; a. 사랑하는; ~에게
You can use dear in expressions such as 'oh dear,' 'dear me,' and 'dear, dear' when you are sad, disappointed, or surprised about something.

teeter [tí:tər] v. 불안정하게 움직이다
If someone or something teeters, they shake in an unsteady way, and seem to be about to lose their balance and fall over.

‡ **steady** [stédi] v. 흔들리지 않다; 진정되다; a. 흔들림 없는, 안정된; 꾸준한
If you steady something or if it steadies, it stops shaking or moving about.

40

* **dart** [daːrt] v. 쏜살같이 움직이다; 흘긋 쳐다보다; n. (작은) 화살; 쏜살같이 달림
If a person or animal darts somewhere, they move there suddenly and quickly.

take hold of idiom ~을 (움켜)잡다
If you take hold of someone or something, you have or take them in your hands.

gain [gein] v. 쌓다, 늘리다; 얻다; n. 증가; 이득
To gain something such as weight or speed means to have an increase in that particular thing.

* **pedal** [pedl] n. 페달, 발판; v. 페달을 밟다; (자전거를) 타고 가다
The pedals on a bicycle are the two parts that you push with your feet in order to make the bicycle move.

yikes [jaiks] int. 이크, 으악
You can say 'yikes' to show that you are worried, surprised, or shocked.

out of breath idiom 숨을 헐떡이며, 숨이 차서
If you are out of breath, you are breathing very quickly and with difficulty because you have been doing something energetic.

* **fool** [fuːl] v. 속이다, 기만하다; n. 바보
If someone fools you, they deceive or trick you.

attention [əténʃən] n. 관심, 흥미; 주의, 주목 (pay attention idiom 관심을 갖다)
If you pay attention to someone, you watch them, listen to them, or take notice of them.

poke [pouk] n. (손가락 등으로) 찌르기; v. (손가락 등으로) 쿡 찌르다; 쑥 내밀다
A poke is a quick push with your finger or a pointed object.

* **rib** [rib] n. 갈비(뼈), 늑골
Your ribs are the 12 pairs of curved bones that surround your chest.

present [preznt] ① a. 현재의; 있는, 존재하는 ② v. 소개하다; 주다; 보여 주다
You use present to describe things and people that exist now, rather than those that existed in the past or those that may exist in the future.

state [steit] n. 상태; 국가; 주(州); v. 말하다, 진술하다
When you talk about the state of someone or something, you are referring to the condition they are in or what they are like at a particular time.

★ **tan** [tæn] v. 햇볕에 타다; 황갈색 (over–tan v. 과하게 햇볕에 타다)
If a part of your body tans or if you tan it, your skin becomes darker than usual because you spend a lot of time in the sun.

★ **detect** [ditékt] v. 발견하다, 알아내다, 감지하다
If you detect something, you notice it or sense it, even though it is not very obvious.

★ **stroll** [stroul] v. 거닐다, 산책하다; n. (한가로이) 거닐기, 산책
If you stroll somewhere, you walk there in a slow, relaxed way.

hand in hand idiom (두 사람이) 서로 손을 잡고
If two people are hand in hand, they are holding each other's nearest hand, usually while they are walking or sitting together.

★ **halt** [hɔːlt] v. 멈추다, 서다; 중단시키다; v. 멈춤, 중단
When a person or a vehicle halts or when something halts them, they stop moving in the direction they were going and stand still.

★ **grove** [grouv] n. (작은) 숲; 밭
A grove is a group of trees that are close together.

‡ **sweetheart** [swíːthàːrt] n. 애인, 연인
Your sweetheart is your boyfriend or your girlfriend.

‡ **propose** [prəpóuz] v. 청혼하다; 제안하다 (proposal n. 청혼)
If you propose to someone, or propose marriage to them, you ask them to marry you.

‡ **marriage** [maéridʒ] n. 결혼 (생활)
A marriage is the relationship between a husband and wife.

courage [kɔ́:ridʒ] n. 용기, 담력
Courage is the quality shown by someone who decides to do something difficult or dangerous, even though they may be afraid.

timid [tímid] a. 소심한, 자신감이 없는
Timid people are shy, nervous, and have no courage or confidence in themselves.

coax [kouks] v. 구슬리다, 달래다
If you coax something such as information out of someone, you gently persuade them to give it to you.

pop [pap] v. 불쑥 내놓다; 펑 하는 소리가 나다; n. 펑 (하는 소리)
(pop the question idiom 청혼하다)
If you pop the question, you ask someone to marry you.

lip [lip] n. 입술
Your lips are the two outer parts of the edge of your mouth.

still [stil] a. 가만히 있는, 정지한; ad. 아직(도) (계속해서)
If you stay still, you stay in the same position and do not move.

value [vǽljuː] v. 소중하게 생각하다; 평가하다; n. 가치, 중요성
If you value something or someone, you think that they are important and you appreciate them.

tremble [trembl] v. (몸을) 떨다; (걱정·두려움으로) 떨리다; n. 떨림, 전율
If you tremble, you shake slightly because you are frightened or cold.

consent [kənsént] v. 동의하다; n. 동의; 합의
If you consent to something, you agree to do it or to allow it to be done.

gulp [gʌlp] v. (공포·놀라움에 질려) 침을 꿀떡 삼기다, 꿀썩꿀썩 삼키다; n. 꿀꺽 마시기
If you gulp, you swallow air, often making a noise in your throat as you do so, because you are nervous or excited.

bite [bait] v. (bit-bit) (이빨로) 물다; 베어 물다; n. 한 입; 물기; 소량
If you bite something, you use your teeth to cut into it, for example in order to eat it or break it.

after all idiom (예상과는 달리) 결국에는; 어쨌든
You use after all when you are saying that something that you thought might not be the case is in fact the case.

* **boring** [bɔ́:riŋ] a. 재미없는, 지루한
Someone or something boring is so dull and uninteresting that they make people tired and impatient.

‡ **conversation** [kànvərséiʃən] n. 대화; 회화
If you have a conversation with someone, you talk with them, usually in an informal situation.

‡‡ **declare** [diklέər] v. 선언하다, 공표하다; 분명히 말하다
If you declare something, you state officially and formally that it exists or is the case.

* **chatter** [ʧǽtər] v. 수다를 떨다, 재잘거리다; n. 수다; 딱딱거리는 소리
If you chatter, you talk quickly and continuously, usually about things which are not important.

‡ **lean** [li:n] v. 기울이다, (몸을) 숙이다; ~에 기대다; a. 호리호리한
When you lean in a particular direction, you bend your body in that direction.

* **faint** [feint] v. 실신하다, 기절하다; n. 실신, 기절
If you faint, you lose consciousness for a short time, especially because you are hungry, or because of pain, heat, or shock.

‡‡ **hardly** [há:rdli] ad. 거의 ~할 수가 없다; 거의 ~아니다; ~하자마자
When you say you can hardly do something, you are emphasizing that it is very difficult for you to do it.

* **embrace** [imbréis] v. 껴안다, 포옹하다; 받아들이다; n. 포옹
If you embrace someone, you put your arms around them and hold them tightly, usually in order to show your love or affection for them.

‡‡ **report** [ripɔ́:rt] v. 알리다, 발표하다, 전하다; (신문·방송에서) 보도하다;
n. 보도; 기록, 보고
If you report something that has happened, you tell people about it.

wed [wed] v. 결혼하다

If one person weds another or if two people wed or are wed, they get married.

★ **glimpse** [glimps] v. 언뜻 보다; 깨닫다, 이해하다; n. 잠깐 봄; 짧은 경험

If you glimpse someone or something, you see them very briefly and not very well.

복습 **pair** [pɛər] n. 두 사람; 한 쌍; v. (둘씩) 짝을 짓다

You can refer to two people as a pair when they are standing or walking together or when they have some kind of relationship with each other.

★ **tease** [tiːz] v. 놀리다, 장난하다; n. 장난, 놀림

To tease someone means to laugh at them or make jokes about them in order to embarrass, annoy, or upset them.

복습 **sneak** [sniːk] v. 살금살금 가다; 몰래 하다; a. 기습적인
(sneak up idiom 살금살금 다가가다)

If sneak up on someone, you approach them very quietly, so that they do not see or hear you until you reach them.

복습 **spy** [spai] v. 염탐하다; (갑자기) 보다, 알아채다; n. 스파이, 정보원

If you spy on someone, you watch them secretly.

The TV Show

1. Why did Stanley agree to go on the TV show?

A. He wanted to meet Teddy Talker.

B. He wanted to make Arthur feel happy.

C. He wanted to share his story with everyone.

D. He wanted to become famous.

2. How did the audience feel when Teddy Talker introduced Arthur?

A. The audience was curious about Arthur's talent.

B. The audience was eager to see Arthur do magic.

C. The audience was not interested in meeting Arthur.

D. The audience was surprised that Arthur was Stanley's brother.

3. How was Arthur able to do the first card trick?

    A. He had Stanley tell him what the chosen card was.

    B. He read Teddy Talker's mind.

    C. He had memorized the order of the cards in the deck.

    D. He used a deck containing one particular card.

4. What did everyone think of Arthur's mind reading and frog magic?

    A. Everyone believed Arthur was very talented.

    B. Everyone was suspicious of Arthur's tricks.

    C. Everyone thought Arthur's tricks were just ordinary.

    D. Everyone felt Arthur's magic was too childish.

5. What did Arthur do before Stanley came onto the stage?

    A. He promised the audience that he could really make frogs fly.

    B. He said he hoped to come back on the show again someday.

    C. He admitted that Stanley had helped him with his tricks.

    D. He talked about his dream of becoming a magician in the future.

Check Your Reading Speed

1분에 몇 단어를 읽는지 리딩 속도를 측정해보세요.

$$\frac{1,659 \text{ words}}{\text{reading time ( ) sec}} \times 60 = (\qquad) \text{ WPM}$$

Build Your Vocabulary

be left out idiom 버려지다
If someone feels left out, they are unhappy because they have not been included in an activity.

✳ **adventure** [ædvénʧər] n. 모험; 모험심
If someone has an adventure, they become involved in an unusual, exciting, and rather dangerous journey or series of events.

복습 **attention** [əténʃən] n. 관심, 흥미; 주의, 주목
If you give someone or something your attention, you look at it, listen to it, or think about it carefully.

✳ **character** [kǽriktər] n. 인격, 품성; 성격, 기질; (책·영화 등의) 등장인물
Your character is your personality, especially how reliable and honest you are.

복습 **cheerful** [ʧíərfəl] a. 발랄한, 쾌활한; 쾌적한 (cheerfulness n. 명랑)
Someone who is cheerful is happy and shows this in their behavior.

✳ **admire** [ædmáiər] v. 존경하다, 칭찬하다; 감탄하며 바라보다
If you admire someone or something, you like and respect them very much.

✳ **wit** [wit] n. 기지, 재치; (pl.) 지혜
Wit is the ability to use words or ideas in an amusing, clever, and imaginative way.

‡ **private** [práivət] a. 은밀한; 사적인; 사유의 (privately ad. 남몰래, 은밀히)
You can use private to describe situations or activities that are understood only by the people involved in them, and not by anyone else.

‡ **jealous** [dʒéləs] a. 질투하는; 시샘하는
If you are jealous of another person's possessions or qualities, you feel angry or bitter because you do not have them.

복습 **stare** [stɛər] v. 빤히 쳐다보다, 응시하다; n. 빤히 쳐다보기, 응시
If you stare at someone or something, you look at them for a long time.

⋆ **sigh** [sai] v. 한숨을 쉬다, 한숨짓다; 탄식하듯 말하다; n. 한숨
When you sigh, you let out a deep breath, as a way of expressing feelings such as disappointment, tiredness, or pleasure.

‡ **cheer** [tʃiər] v. 응원하다, 힘을 북돋우다; 환호하다; n. 환호
If you are cheered by something, it makes you happier or less worried.

⋆ **host** [houst] n. (TV · 라디오 프로그램의) 진행자; 주인; v. 주최하다; (프로그램을) 진행하다
The host of a radio or television show is the person who introduces it and talks to the people who appear in it.

복습 **enormous** [inɔ́ːrməs] a. 막대한, 거대한 (enormously ad. 엄청나게, 대단히)
Something that is enormous is extremely large in size or amount.

‡ **particular** [pərtíkjulər] a. 특별한; 특정한; 까다로운 (particularly ad. 특히, 특별히)
Particularly means more than usual or more than other things.

복습 **joke** [dʒouk] n. 농담; 웃음거리; v. 농담하다; 농담삼아 말하다
A joke is something that is said or done to make you laugh, for example a funny story.

‡ **trick** [trik] n. 마술; 장난, 속임수; v. 속이다, 속임수를 쓰다
A trick is a clever or skillful action that someone does in order to entertain people.

⋆ **pleased** [pliːzd] a. 기쁜, 기뻐하는, 만족해하는
If you are pleased, you are happy about something or satisfied with something.

‡ **stage** [steidʒ] n. 무대; 시기, 단계; v. 개최하다, 무대에 올리다
In a theater, the stage is an area where actors or other entertainers perform.

복습 **include** [inklúːd] v. 포함하다; ~을 (~에) 포함시키다
If one thing includes another thing, it has the other thing as one of its parts.

★ **row** [rou] n. 열, 줄; 노 젓기; v. 노를 젓다
A row of things or people is a number of them arranged in a line.

★ **applaud** [əplɔ́ːd] v. 박수를 치다; 갈채를 보내다
When a group of people applaud, they clap their hands in order to show approval, for example when they have enjoyed a play or concert.

복습 **rest** [rest] n. 나머지; 휴식; v. 쉬다; 놓이다, (~에) 있다
The rest is used to refer to all the parts of something or all the things in a group that remain or that you have not already mentioned.

‡ **audience** [ɔ́ːdiəns] n. 청중, 관중; 접견
The audience at a play, concert, film, or public meeting is the group of people watching or listening to it.

‡‡ **dress** [dres] v. 옷을 입다; n. 드레스; 옷 (dressing room n. 분장실)
A dressing room is a room in a theater where performers can dress and get ready for their performance.

backstage [bækstéidʒ] ad. 무대 뒤에서; 은밀히
In a theater, backstage refers to the areas behind the stage.

★ **chat** [ʧæt] v. 이야기를 나누다, 수다를 떨다; n. 이야기, 대화
When people chat, they talk to each other in an informal and friendly way.

★ **champion** [ʧǽmpiən] n. 챔피언, 대회 우승자
A champion is someone who has won the first prize in a competition, contest, or fight.

* contest [kántest] ① n. 대회, 시합 ② v. 이의를 제기하다; 경쟁을 벌이다
A contest is a competition or game in which people try to win.

⁂ devote [divóut] v. (~에) 바치다, 쏟다, 기울이다
If you devote yourself, your time, or your energy to something, you spend all or most of your time or energy on it.

⁑ cause [kɔːz] n. (정치·사회적 운동) 조직; 원인; 이유; v. ~을 야기하다
A cause is an aim or principle which a group of people supports or is fighting for.

⁑ announce [ənáuns] v. 발표하다, 알리다; 선언하다 (announcement n. 발표)
An announcement is a statement made to the public or to the media which gives information about something that has happened or that will happen.

⁑ delay [diléi] v. 미루다, 연기하다; 지연시키다; n. 지연, 지체; 연기
If you delay doing something, you do not do it immediately or at the planned or expected time, but you leave it until later.

* meanwhile [míːnwàil] ad. 그동안에
Meanwhile means in the period of time between two events.

⁑ fortunate [fɔ́ːrʧənət] a. 운 좋은, 다행한
If you say that someone or something is fortunate, you mean that they are lucky.

복습 talented [tǽləntid] a. 재능이 있는
Someone who is talented has a natural ability to do something well.

⁑ protest [próutest] n. 항의; 시위; v. 항의하다, 이의를 제기하다
A protest is the act of saying or showing publicly that you object to something.

mirth [məːr] n. 웃음소리, 즐거움
Mirth is amusement which you express by laughing.

⁑ smart [smaːrt] a. 단정한, 멋있는; 똑똑한, 영리한
Smart people and things are pleasantly neat and clean in appearance.

★ **magician** [mədʒíʃən] n. 마술사; 마법사
A magician is a person who entertains people by doing magic tricks.

★ **cape** [keip] n. 망토
A cape is a short cloak, which is a long, loose, sleeveless piece of clothing.

★ **well** [wel] n. 우물; 근원; v. (액체가) 솟아 나오다, 샘솟다; int. 이런, 이거 참
A well is a hole in the ground from which a supply of water is extracted.

★ **riddle** [ridl] n. 수수께끼; v. 구멍을 숭숭 뚫다
A riddle is a puzzle or joke in which you ask a question that seems to be nonsense but which has a clever or amusing answer.

‡ **army** [á:rmi] n. 군대
An army is a large organized group of people who are armed and trained to fight on land in a war.

★ **sleeve** [sli:v] n. (옷의) 소매, 소맷자락
The sleeves of a coat, shirt, or other item of clothing are the parts that cover your arms.

shuffle [ʃʌfl] v. (카드를) 섞다; 발을 끌며 걷다; n. 느릿느릿 걷기; (카드를) 섞기
If you shuffle playing cards, you mix them up before you begin a game.

★ **deck** [dek] n. (카드) 한 벌; 갑판
A deck of cards is a complete set of playing cards.

‡ **concentrate** [kánsəntrèit] v. (정신을) 집중하다; (한 곳에) 모으다; n. 농축물
If you concentrate on something, or concentrate your mind on it, you give all your attention to it.

★ **incredible** [inkrédəbl] a. 믿을 수 없는, 믿기 힘든
If you say that something is incredible, you mean that it is very unusual or surprising, and you cannot believe it is really true, although it may be.

복습 **lad** [læd] n. 사내애; 청년
A lad is a young man or boy.

tie [tai] v. (끈 등으로) 묶다; 결부시키다; n. 끈; 유대
If you tie two things together or tie them, you fasten them together with a knot.

volunteer [vàləntíər] n. 자원하는 사람; 자원 봉사자; v. 자원하다; 제안하다
A volunteer is someone who offers to do a particular task or job without being forced to do it.

elderly [éldərli] a. 나이가 지긋한
You use elderly as a polite way of saying that someone is old.

tiptoe [típtòu] v. (발끝으로) 살금살금 걷다
If you tiptoe somewhere, you walk there very quietly without putting your heels on the floor when you walk.

peculiar [pikjú:ljər] a. 이상한, 기이한; 고유한
If you describe someone or something as peculiar, you think that they are strange or unusual, sometimes in an unpleasant way.

peek [pi:k] n. 엿보기; v. 살짝 보이다; (재빨리) 훔쳐보다
A peek is a quick look at something, especially secretly or from behind something.

whisper [hwíspər] v. 속삭이다, 소곤거리다; n. 속삭임, 소곤거리는 소리
When you whisper, you say something very quietly, using your breath rather than your throat, so that only one person can hear you.

bravo [brá:vou] int. 브라보!, 잘한다!
Some people say 'bravo' to express appreciation when someone has done something well.

clap [klæp] v. 박수를 치다; (갑자기·재빨리) 놓다; n. 박수; 쿵 하는 소리
When you clap, you hit your hands together to show appreciation or attract attention.

clever [klévər] a. 기발한, 재치 있는; 영리한, 똑똑한
A clever idea, book, or invention is extremely effective and shows the skill of the people involved.

draw a breath idiom 깊이 숨쉬다, 심호흡하다
If you draw a deep breath, you breathe in deeply once.

pet [pet] n. 애완동물; v. (다정하게) 어루만지다
A pet is an animal that you keep in your home to give you company and pleasure.

next door [nekst dɔ́:r] ad. 옆집에(서); n. 옆집 사람
If a room or building is next door, it is the next one to the right or left.

dare [dɛər] v. 감히 ~하다, ~할 용기가 있다; 부추기다; n. 모험, 도전 (daring a. 대담한)
A daring person is willing to do things that might be dangerous.

still [stil] a. 가만히 있는, 정지한; ad. 아직(도) (계속해서)
If you stay still, you stay in the same position and do not move.

wriggle [rigl] v. (몸을) 꿈틀거리다; 꿈틀거리며 가다; n. 꿈틀거리기
If you wriggle or wriggle part of your body, you twist and turn with quick movements, for example because you are uncomfortable.

amaze [əméiz] v. (대단히) 놀라게 하다 (amazing a. 놀라운)
You say that something is amazing when it is very surprising and makes you feel pleasure, approval, or wonder.

circle [sə́:rkl] v. 빙빙 돌다; 에워싸다, 둘러싸다; n. 원형
If an aircraft or a bird circles or circles something, it moves round in a circle in the air.

command [kəmǽnd] v. 명령하다, 지시하다; n. 명령; 지휘, 통솔
If someone in authority commands you to do something, they tell you that you must do it.

rapid [rǽpid] a. (속도가) 빠른; (행동이) 민첩한 (rapidly ad. 빠르게, 신속히)
A rapid movement is one that is very fast.

sway [swei] v. (전후·좌우로) 흔들다; (마음을) 동요시키다; n. 흔들림
When people or things sway, they lean or swing slowly from one side to the other.

tremendous [triméndəs] a. 엄청난; 굉장한, 대단한 (tremendously ad. 엄청나게)
You use tremendous to emphasize how strong a feeling or quality is, or how large an amount is.

impress [imprés] v. 깊은 인상을 주다, 감동을 주다 (impressed a. 감명을 받은)
If something impresses you, you feel great admiration for it.

swoop [swuːp] v. 급강하하다, 위에서 덮치다; 급습하다; n. 급강하; 급습
When a bird or airplane swoops, it suddenly moves downward through the air in a smooth curving movement.

duck [dʌk] v. (머리나 몸을) 휙 수그리다; 급히 움직이다; n. [동물] 오리
If you duck, you move your head or the top half of your body quickly downward to avoid something that might hit you, or to avoid being seen.

sight [sait] n. 광경, 모습; 시야; 보기, 봄; v. 갑자기 보다
A sight is something that you see.

applause [əplɔ́ːz] n. 박수 (갈채)
Applause is the noise made by a group of people clapping their hands to show approval.

whoosh [hwuːʃ] v. (아주 빠르게) 휙 하고 지나가다; n. 쉭 하는 소리
If something whooshes somewhere, it moves there quickly or suddenly.

terrible [térəbl] a. 극심한; 끔찍한, 소름끼치는; 형편없는 (terribly ad. 몹시, 극심하게)
You use terrible to emphasize the great extent or degree of something.

confuse [kənfjúːz] v. (사람을) 혼란시키다; 혼동하다 (confused a. 혼란스러워 하는)
If you are confused, you do not know exactly what is happening or what to do.

squirrel [skwə́ːrəl] n. [동물] 다람쥐
A squirrel is a small animal with a long furry tail.

go on idiom 말을 계속하다; (상황이) 계속되다
To go on means to continue speaking after a short pause.

spring [spriŋ] v. (sprang-sprung) 휙 움직이다; (갑자기) 뛰어오르다; n. 봄; 생기, 활기; 샘
When a person or animal springs, they jump upward or forward suddenly or quickly.

present [prizént] ① v. 소개하다; 주다; 보여 주다 ② a. 있는, 존재하는; 현재의; n. 선물
If you present someone to someone else, often an important person, you formally introduce them.

all along idiom 내내, 죽
If something has been true or been present all along, it has been true or been present throughout a period of time.

bow [bau] v. (허리를 굽혀) 절하다; n. 절, (고개 숙여 하는) 인사
When you bow to someone, you briefly bend your body toward them as a formal way of greeting them or showing respect.

bob [bab] v. 위아래로 움직이다; (고개를) 까닥거리다; n. (머리·몸을) 까닥거림
If something bobs, it moves up and down, like something does when it is floating on water.

plain [plein] a. (보거나 이해하기에) 분명한; 솔직한
If a fact, situation, or statement is plain, it is easy to recognize or understand.

theatrical [θiǽtrikəl] a. 연극의, 연극적인
Theatrical can be used to describe something that is grand and dramatic, as if it is part of a performance in a theater.

flair [flɛər] n. 솜씨, 재간; 재주
If you have flair, you do things in an original, interesting, and stylish way.

treat [triːt] n. 기쁨; (대접하는) 특별한 것; v. (특정한 태도로) 대하다; 치료하다; 대접하다
A treat is a special and enjoyable occasion or experience.

bump [bʌmp] v. (~에) 부딪치다; 덜컹거리며 가다; n. 부딪치기; 쿵, 탁 (하는 소리)
If you bump into something or someone, you accidentally hit them while you are moving.

^{복습}**remind** [rimáind] v. 상기시키다, 다시 한 번 알려 주다

If someone reminds you of a fact or event that you already know about, they say something which makes you think about it.

poise [pɔiz] n. 침착; (몸의) 균형; v. 태세를 취하다

If someone has poise, they are calm, dignified, and self-controlled.

contribute [kəntríbju:t] v. 기여하다; (~의) 원인이 되다; 기부하다

If you contribute to something, you say or do things to help to make it successful.

count [kaunt] n. 사항; 셈, 계산; 수치; v. 중요하다; 간주하다; (수를) 세다

You can use count to refer to one or more points that you are considering.

The Bank Robbers

1. **Why did Stanley go into the ice cream van?**

   A. He figured Mr. Lambchop would be able to find him there later.

   B. He was hoping there would be some ice cream to eat there.

   C. He thought he would be safe from the robbers there.

   D. He planned to stay there and follow the robbers.

2. **What did the robbers do first when they got inside the van?**

   A. They checked that no one else was in the van.

   B. They hid the stolen money in one of the barrels.

   C. They turned on the van and sped off.

   D. They put on their wigs and dresses.

3. How did the tall robber react when the policeman said a bank had been robbed?

   A. He claimed he had seen some suspicious-looking females nearby.

   B. He said he already knew about the bank being robbed.

   C. He became very nervous and shaky.

   D. He acted surprised by the news.

4. Why did Stanley flip the lids off the barrels?

   A. To show the policemen that the two men were the robbers

   B. To scare the robbers so that they would confess about the stolen money

   C. To make the policemen and robbers aware of his presence

   D. To find out what was inside the barrels

5. How was Mr. Lambchop able to find Stanley?

   A. He had heard where Stanley was from a policeman.

   B. He had seen Stanley get into the van.

   C. He had heard Stanley talking in the van.

   D. He had followed Stanley's balloon caught in the van.

Check Your Reading Speed

1분에 몇 단어를 읽는지 리딩 속도를 측정해보세요.

$$\frac{982 \text{ words}}{\text{reading time ( ) sec}} \times 60 = (\quad) \text{ WPM}$$

Build Your Vocabulary

⚹ rob [rab] v. (사람·장소를) 도둑질하다 (robber n. 강도)

A robber is someone who steals money or property from a bank, a shop, or a vehicle, often by using force or threats.

⚹ dreadful [drédfəl] a. 무시무시한; 끔찍한, 지독한

If you say that something is dreadful, you mean that it is very bad or unpleasant, or very poor in quality.

⚹ scandal [skǽndl] n. 추문, 스캔들; 남부끄러운 일

A scandal is a situation or event that is thought to be shocking and immoral and that everyone knows about.

⚹ violent [váiələnt] a. 폭력적인; 맹렬한; 지독한 (violence n. 폭행, 폭력)

Violence is behavior which is intended to hurt, injure, or kill people.

newscaster [njúːzkæstər] n. (라디오·텔레비전의) 뉴스 프로그램 진행자

A newscaster is a person who reads the news on the radio or on television.

복습 report [ripɔ́ːrt] n. 보도; 기록, 보고;

v. (신문·방송에서) 보도하다; 알리다, 발표하다, 전하다

A report is a news article or broadcast which gives information about something that has just happened.

⚹ affair [əféər] n. 일, 문제; 사건; 업무

You can use affairs to refer to all the important facts or activities that are connected with a particular subject.

crime [kraim] n. 범죄, 죄
A crime is an illegal action or activity for which a person can be punished by law.

bustle [bʌsl] v. 바삐 움직이다, 서두르다; n. 부산함, 북적거림
If someone bustles somewhere, they move there in a hurried way, often because they are very busy.

switch off idiom (스위치 등을 눌러서) ~을 끄다
If you switch off something like an electrical device, a machine or an engine, you stop it working by pressing a switch or a button.

stroll [stroul] v. 거닐다, 산책하다; n. (한가로이) 거닐기, 산책
If you stroll somewhere, you walk there in a slow, relaxed way.

cash [kæʃ] v. 수표를 현금으로 바꾸다; n. 현금
If you cash a check, you exchange it at a bank for the amount of money that it is worth.

check [ʧek] n. 수표; 확인, 점검; v. 살피다, 점검하다
A check is a printed form on which you write an amount of money and who it is to be paid to.

crowd [kraud] v. 가득 메우다; (생각이 마음속에) 밀려오다; n. 사람들, 군중
(crowded a. 붐비는)
If a place is crowded, it is full of people.

fancy [fǽnsi] a. 장식이 많은, 색깔이 화려한; 고급의; v. 생각하다, 상상하다
If you describe something as fancy, you mean that it is special, unusual, or elaborate, for example because it has a lot of decoration.

stout [staut] a. 통통한; 튼튼한
A stout person is rather fat.

pistol [pístəl] n. 권총, 피스톨
A pistol is a small gun which is held in and fired from one hand.

scratch [skrætʃ] v. (가려운 데를) 긁다; 긁힌 자국을 내다; n. 긁는 소리; 긁힌 자국
(scratchy a. 긁는 듯한 소리가 나는)
Scratchy sounds are thin and harsh.

bang [bæŋ] n. 쾅 (하는 소리); v. 쾅 하고 치다; 쾅 하고 닫다; 쿵 하고 찧다
A bang is a sudden loud noise such as the noise of an explosion.

odd [ad] a. 이상한, 특이한; 홀수의
If you describe someone or something as odd, you think that they are
strange or unusual.

shoot [ʃuːt] v. (총 등을) 쏘다; 휙 움직이다
If someone shoots a person or an animal, they kill them or injure them
by firing a bullet or arrow at them.

visible [vízəbl] a. (눈에) 보이는, 알아볼 수 있는; 뚜렷한 (invisible a. 보이지 않는)
If you describe something as invisible, you mean that it cannot be seen,
for example because it is transparent, hidden, or very small.

protect [prətékt] v. 보호하다, 지키다; 보장하다
To protect someone or something means to prevent them from being
harmed or damaged.

bullet [búlit] n. 총알
A bullet is a small piece of metal with a pointed or rounded end, which
is fired out of a gun.

yum-yum [jʌm-jʌ́m] int. 냠냠
People sometimes say 'yum' or 'yum-yum' to show that they think
something tastes or smells very good.

van [væn] n. 승합차; 밴
A van is a small or medium-sized road vehicle with one row of seats at
the front and a space for carrying goods behind.

float [flout] v. (물 위나 공중에서) 떠가다; (물에) 뜨다; n. 부표
Something that floats in or through the air hangs in it or moves slowly
and gently through it.

string [striŋ] n. 끈, 줄; 일련; v. 묶다, 매달다; (실 등에) 꿰다
String is thin rope made of twisted threads, used for tying things together or tying up parcels.

dare [dɛər] v. 감히 ~하다, ~할 용기가 있다; 부추기다; n. 모험, 도전
If you do not dare to do something, you do not have enough courage to do it, or you do not want to do it because you fear the consequences.

* **rescue** [réskjuː] v. 구하다, 구출하다; n. 구출, 구조, 구제
To rescue something means to keep it from being lost or abandoned.

scrunch [skrʌntʃ] v. 웅크리다; 뿌드득뿌드득 소리를 내다
If you scrunch something or yourself, you make it or yourself smaller to fit into a small space.

* **cardboard** [káːrdbɔːrd] n. 판지
Cardboard is thick, stiff paper that is used, for example, to make boxes and models.

* **barrel** [bǽrəl] n. (대형) 통; v. 쏜살같이 달리다
A barrel is a large, round container for liquids or food.

mark [maːrk] v. 표시하다; 자국을 내다; n. 자국, 흔적
If you mark something with a particular word or symbol, you write that word or symbol on it.

crunch [krʌntʃ] n. 으드득 (하는 소리); v. 으드득거리다; 저벅저벅거리며 가다
The crunch is the loud noise that something hard makes when you bite it.

peek [piːk] v. (재빨리) 훔쳐보다; 살짝 보이다; n. 엿보기
If you peek at something or someone, you have a quick look at them, often secretly.

* **alarm** [əláːrm] n. 경보 장치; 불안, 공포; v. 불안하게 하다; 경보장치를 달다
An alarm is an automatic device that warns you of danger, for example by ringing a bell.

hold one's breath idiom (흥분·공포 등으로) 숨을 죽이다
If you say that someone is holding their breath, you mean that they are
waiting anxiously or excitedly for something to happen.

pour [pɔːr] v. 마구 쏟아지다; 붓다, 따르다
If you pour a liquid or other substance, you make it flow steadily out of
a container by holding the container at an angle.

packet [pǽkit] n. 소포; 한 묶음; 통, 갑
A packet is a small flat parcel.

lid [lid] n. 뚜껑
A lid is the top of a box or other container which can be removed or
raised when you want to open the container.

hardly [háːrdli] ad. 거의 ~할 수가 없다; 거의 ~아니다; ~하자마자
When you say you can hardly do something, you are emphasizing that
it is very difficult for you to do it.

tug [tʌg] v. (세게) 잡아당기다; n. (갑자기 세게) 잡아당김
If you tug something or tug at it, you give it a quick and usually strong
pull.

wig [wig] n. 가발
A wig is a covering of false hair which you wear on your head.

dress [dres] v. 옷을 입다; n. 드레스; 옷 (undress v. 옷을 벗다)
When you undress or undress someone, you take off your clothes or
someone else's clothes.

realize [ríːəlàiz] v. 깨닫다, 알아차리다; 실현하다, 달성하다
If you realize that something is true, you become aware of that fact or
understand it.

underneath [ʌndərníːθ] prep. ~의 밑에, ~의 안에
If one thing is underneath another, it is directly under it, and may be
covered or hidden by it.

roll [roul] v. 걷어 올리다; (둥글게) 말다; 구르다; n. 뒹굴기; 구르기
If you roll your sleeves or the legs of your trousers up, you fold the cloth several times until they are shorter.

relieve [rilíːv] v. 안도하게 하다; (불쾌감·고통 등을) 없애 주다; 완화하다
(relief n. 안도, 안심)
If you feel a sense of relief, you feel happy because something unpleasant has not happened or is no longer happening.

kick off idiom (신발 등을) 차서 벗다
If you kick your shoes off, you make them come off by shaking your feet.

sneaker [sníːkər] n. (pl.) 운동화
Sneakers are casual shoes with rubber soles.

trouser [tráuzər] n. 바지의 한쪽; (pl.) 바지
A trouser leg is a cloth covering consisting of the part of a pair of trousers.

speed [spiːd] v. (sped–sped) 빨리 가다; 더 빠르게 하다; n. 속도
If you speed somewhere, you move or travel there quickly, usually in a vehicle.

pair [pɛər] n. 두 사람; 한 쌍; v. (둘씩) 짝을 짓다
You can refer to two people as a pair when they are standing or walking together or when they have some kind of relationship with each other.

clever [klévər] a. 기발한, 재치 있는; 영리한, 똑똑한
A clever idea, book, or invention is extremely effective and shows the skill of the people involved.

get away idiom 도망치다; ~로부터 벗어나다; 휴가를 가다
If you get away from someone or somewhere, you escape from them or there.

suspect [səspékt] v. 의심하다; 수상쩍어 하다; n. 용의자
If you suspect someone of doing an action of this kind, you believe that they probably did it.

block [blak] v. 막다, 차단하다; 방해하다; n. 구역, 블록; 사각형 덩어리
To block a road, channel, or pipe means to put an object across it or in it so that nothing can pass through it or along it.

policeman [pəlíːsmən] n. (pl. policemen) 경찰관
A policeman is a person who is a member of the police force.

inspect [inspékt] v. 점검하다, 검사하다
If you inspect something, you look at every part of it carefully in order to find out about it or check that it is all right.

fellow [félou] n. 녀석, 친구; 동료; a. 동료의
A fellow is a man or boy.

suspicious [səspíʃəs] a. 의심스러운; 의혹을 갖는, 수상쩍어 하는
If you describe someone or something as suspicious, you mean that there is some aspect of them which makes you think that they are involved in a crime or a dishonest activity.

fill [fil] v. (일·역할 등을) 하다; (가득) 채우다; (구멍·틈을) 때우다
If something fills a role, position, or function, they have that role or position, or perform that function, often successfully.

role [roul] n. 역할; 배역
If you have a role in a situation or in society, you have a particular position and function in it.

bless [bles] v. (신의) 축복을 빌다
Bless is used in expressions such as 'bless you' or 'God bless' to express affection, thanks, or good wishes.

hasty [héisti] a. 서두른; 성급한 (hastily ad. 급히, 서둘러서)
A hasty movement, action, or statement is sudden, and often done in reaction to something that has just happened.

trickery [tríkəri] n. 속임수, 사기
Trickery is the use of dishonest methods in order to achieve something.

reach [riːʃ] v. (손·팔을) 뻗다; ~에 이르다; n. (닿을 수 있는) 거리; 범위
If you can reach something, you are able to touch it by stretching out your arm or leg.

flip [flip] v. 홱 뒤집다, 휙 젖히다; 톡 던지다; n. 톡 던지기
If something flips over, or if you flip it over or into a different position, it moves or is moved into a different position.

loose [luːs] a. 풀린, 헐거운; 꽉 죄지 않는
Something that is loose is not firmly held or fixed in place.

tighten [taitn] v. (더 단단히) 조이다; (더) 팽팽해지다; 더 엄격하게 하다
When you tighten a screw, nut, or other device, you turn it or move it so that it is more firmly in place or holds something more firmly.

needy [níːdi] a. (경제적으로) 어려운, 궁핍한
Needy people do not have enough food, medicine, or clothing, or adequate houses.

late [leit] a. 고인이 된, 이미 사망한; 늦은
You use late when you are talking about someone who is dead, especially someone who has died recently.

plain [plein] a. (보거나 이해하기에) 분명한; 솔직한
If a fact, situation, or statement is plain, it is easy to recognize or understand.

mighty [máiti] ad. 대단히, 굉장히; a. 강력한, 힘센
Mighty is used in front of adjectives and adverbs to emphasize the quality that they are describing.

handcuff [hǽndkʌ̀f] v. 수갑을 채우다; n. 수갑
If you handcuff someone, you put handcuffs around their wrists.

confuse [kənfjúːz] v. (사람을) 혼란시키다; 혼동하다 (confused a. 혼란스러워 하는)
If you are confused, you do not know exactly what is happening or what to do.

* **yell** [jel] v. 고함치다, 소리 지르다; n. 고함, 외침
If you yell, you shout loudly, usually because you are excited, angry, or in pain.

‡ **unfortunately** [ʌnfɔ́ːrtʃənətli] ad. 불행하게도, 유감스럽게도
You can use unfortunately to introduce or refer to a statement when you consider that it is sad or disappointing, or when you want to express regret.

thank goodness idiom 정말 다행이다
You say 'thank God' or 'thank goodness' when you are very relieved about something.

* **groan** [groun] v. 끙끙거리다; (고통·짜증으로) 신음을 내다; n. 신음, 끙 하는 소리
If you groan something, you say it in a low, unhappy voice.

* **shrug** [ʃrʌg] v. (어깨를) 으쓱하다; n. 어깨를 으쓱하기
If you shrug, you raise your shoulders to show that you are not interested in something or that you do not know or care about something.

‡ **blame** [bleim] v. ~을 탓하다, ~의 책임으로 보다; n. 책임; 탓
If you blame a person or thing for something bad, you believe or say that they are responsible for it or that they caused it.

* **jail** [dʒeil] n. 교도소, 감옥; v. 수감하다
A jail is a place where criminals are kept in order to punish them, or where people waiting to be tried are kept.

‡ **cab** [kæb] n. 택시
A cab is a taxi.

Arthur's Storm

1. **What was one reason that Stanley didn't want to be invisible anymore?**

   A. He didn't like all the attention he was getting.

   B. He didn't like having to carry around a balloon.

   C. People didn't listen to him well anymore.

   D. People didn't want to talk to him anymore.

2. **What was Arthur's idea for making Stanley normal again?**

   A. Recreating the same situation as the night Stanley became invisible

   B. Waiting for a real storm to strike again

   C. Having Stanley eat different fruit from those that he had eaten before

   D. Making Stanley eat fruit while standing in the shower

3. **What did Mrs. Lambchop use the wooden spoon and skillet for?**

   A. She used them to make the sound of thunder.

   B. She used them to make the sound of lightning.

   C. She used them to make the sound of rain.

   D. She used them to cook the apple and raisins.

4. **Why did Arthur tell Stanley to twist around?**

   A. He wanted to check that Stanley could move okay.

   B. He wanted to make Stanley dizzy.

   C. He thought it might help change Stanley.

   D. He thought it would make everything more exciting.

5. **When did Stanley finally start to become visible again?**

   A. After the Lambchops turned off the water in the bathroom

   B. After the Lambchops turned on the lights in the room

   C. After he finished eating the apple

   D. After he finished eating all the raisins

Check Your Reading Speed

1분에 몇 단어를 읽는지 리딩 속도를 측정해보세요.

$$\frac{1,166 \text{ words}}{\text{reading time ( ) sec}} \times 60 = (\qquad) \text{ WPM}$$

Build Your Vocabulary

storm [stɔːrm] n. 폭풍; v. 폭풍이 불다; 쿵쾅대며 가다

A storm is very bad weather, with heavy rain, strong winds, and often thunder and lightning.

yawn [jɔːn] v. 하품하다; n. 하품

If you yawn, you open your mouth very wide and breathe in more air than usual, often when you are tired or when you are not interested in something.

pleasant [plézənt] a. 즐거운, 기분 좋은; 상냥한

Something that is pleasant is nice, enjoyable, or attractive.

rob [rab] v. (사람 · 장소를) 도둑질하다 (robber n. 강도)

A robber is someone who steals money or property from a bank, a shop, or a vehicle, often by using force or threats.

shoot [ʃuːt] v. (shot–shot) (총 등을) 쏘다; 휙 움직이다

If someone shoots a person or an animal, they kill them or injure them by firing a bullet or arrow at them.

by accident idiom 우연히

If you say that something happens by accident, you mean that it has not been planned.

sigh [sai] v. 한숨을 쉬다, 한숨짓다; 탄식하듯 말하다; n. 한숨

When you sigh, you let out a deep breath, as a way of expressing feelings such as disappointment, tiredness, or pleasure.

72

^{복습} **go on** idiom (상황이) 계속되다; 말을 계속하다

To go on means to continue to happen or exist without changing.

^{복습} **visible** [vízəbl] a. (눈에) 보이는, 알아볼 수 있는; 뚜렷한 (invisible a. 보이지 않는)

If you describe something as invisible, you mean that it cannot be seen, for example because it is transparent, hidden, or very small.

[*] **scare** [skɛər] v. 무서워하다; 놀라게 하다; n. 불안(감); 놀람, 공포

(scared a. 무서워하는, 겁먹은)

If you are scared that something unpleasant might happen, you are nervous and worried because you think that it might happen.

^{복습} **bump** [bʌmp] v. (~에) 부딪치다; 덜컹거리며 가다; n. 부딪치기; 쿵, 탁 (하는 소리)

If you bump into something or someone, you accidentally hit them while you are moving.

laugh at idiom ~을 비웃다, 놀리다

If people laugh at someone or something, they mock them or make jokes about them.

^{**} **fix** [fiks] n. 곤경; 해결책; v. 고정시키다; 수리하다

A fix can refer to a difficult situation or a big problem.

^{복습} **tremble** [trembl] n. 떨림, 전율; v. (몸을) 떨다; (걱정·두려움으로) 떨다

A tremble is a slight shake.

[*] **edge** [edʒ] n. 끝, 가장자리; 우위; v. 조금씩 움직이다; 테두리를 두르다

The edge of something is the place or line where it stops, or the part of it that is furthest from the middle.

^{복습} **beneath** [biníːθ] prep. 아래에; ~보다 못한

Something that is beneath another thing is under the other thing.

^{복습} **cover** [kʌvər] n. 덮개, 커버; 몸을 숨길 곳; v. (감추거나 보호하기 위해) 씌우다; 덮다

The covers on your bed are the things such as sheets and blankets that you have on top of you.

＊pat [pæt] v. 가볍게 두드리다; 쓰다듬다; n. 쓰다듬기, 토닥거리기

If you pat something or someone, you tap them lightly, usually with your hand held flat.

＊knock [nak] n. 문 두드리는 소리; 부딪침; v. 치다, 부딪치다; (문 등을) 두드리다

A knock is a sudden short noise made when someone or something hits a surface.

＊wave [weiv] v. (손·팔을) 흔들다; 흔들리다; n. 파도, 물결; (손·팔을) 흔들기

If you wave something, you hold it up and move it rapidly from side to side.

복습dear [diər] n. 얘야; 여보, 당신; int. 이런!, 맙소사!; a. 사랑하는; ~에게

You can call someone dear as a sign of affection.

복습sight [sait] n. 시야; 광경, 모습; 보기, 봄; v. 갑자기 보다

(out of sight, out of mind idiom 눈에 보이지 않으면 곧 잊혀진다)

If something is out of sight, you cannot see it.

＊saying [séiiŋ] n. 속담, 격언

A saying is a sentence that people often say and that gives advice or information about human life and experience.

＊awful [ɔ́:fəl] a. 끔찍한, 지독한; (정도가) 대단한, 아주 심한

If you say that something is awful, you mean that it is extremely unpleasant, shocking, or bad.

＊cure [kjuər] n. 치유법; 해결책; v. 낫게 하다

A cure for an illness is a medicine or other treatment that cures the illness.

복습connection [kənékʃən] n. 관련성; 연결, 접속

A connection is a relationship between two things, people, or groups.

복습except [iksépt] prep. 제외하고는

You use except for to introduce the only thing or person that prevents a statement from being completely true.

‡ **nod** [nad] v. (고개를) 끄덕이다, 까딱하다; n. (고개를) 끄덕임
If you nod, you move your head downward and upward to show that you are answering 'yes' to a question, or to show agreement, understanding, or approval.

‡ **harm** [ha:rm] n. 해, 피해, 손해; v. 해치다; 손상시키다
(no harm in something idiom ~해서 나쁠 건 없다)
If you say there is no harm in doing something, you mean that it might be worth doing, and you will not be blamed for doing it.

‡ **gather** [gǽðər] v. (여기저기 있는 것을) 모으다; (사람들이) 모이다
If you gather things, you collect them together so that you can use them.

‡ **require** [rikwáiər] v. 필요로 하다, 요구하다
If you require something or if something is required, you need it or it is necessary.

* **stripe** [straip] n. 줄무늬; v. 줄무늬를 넣다 (stripey a. 줄무늬가 있는)
Something that is stripey has stripes on it.

‡ **pajamas** [pədʒá:məz] n. (바지와 상의로 된) 잠옷
A pair of pajamas consists of loose trousers and a loose jacket that people, especially men, wear in bed.

‡ **run** [rʌn] v. (ran–run) (물을) 받다; 달리다; n. 달리기
If you run water, or if you run a tap or a bath, you cause water to flow from a tap.

‡ **sink** [siŋk] n. 세면기; (부엌의) 싱크대; v. 가라앉다; 침몰시키다
A sink is the same as a washbasin, which is a large bowl, usually with taps for hot and cold water, for washing your hands and face.

* **wooden** [wudn] a. 나무로 된, 목재의; 경직된
Wooden objects are made of wood.

skillet [skílit] n. 프라이팬
A skillet is a shallow iron pan which is used for frying.

복습 **thunder** [θʌ́ndər] n. 천둥; v. 천둥이 치다; 우르릉거리다
Thunder is the loud noise that you hear from the sky after a flash of lightning, especially during a storm.

⁎ **flashlight** [flǽʃlait] n. 손전등
A flashlight is a small electric light which gets its power from batteries and which you can carry in your hand.

복습 **fetch** [feʧ] v. 가지고 오다, 데리고 오다; (특정 가격에) 팔리다; n. 가져옴, 데려옴
If you fetch something or someone, you go and get them from the place where they are.

⁎ **tool** [tuːl] n. 도구, 연장
A tool is any instrument or simple piece of equipment that you hold in your hands and use to do a particular kind of work.

⁎ **kit** [kit] n. (도구·장비) 세트; 조립용품 세트
A kit is a group of items that are kept together, often in the same container, because they are all used for similar purposes.

복습 **lightning** [láitniŋ] n. 번개, 번갯불; a. 아주 빨리; 급작스럽게
Lightning is the very bright flashes of light in the sky that happen during thunderstorms.

put out idiom (불을) 끄다; 내쫓다
To put out a light means to make it stop shining by pressing or moving a switch.

복습 **whoosh** [hwuːʃ] n. 쉭 하는 소리; v. (아주 빠르게) 휙 하고 지나가다
People sometimes say 'whoosh' when they are emphasizing the fact that something happens very suddenly or very fast.

patter [pǽtər] v. 후두두 하는 소리를 내다; n. 후두두 하는 소리
If something patters on a surface, it hits it quickly several times, making quiet, tapping sounds.

⁎ **tub** [tʌb] n. 욕조; 통
A tub is a long, usually rectangular container which you fill with water and sit in to wash your body.

‡‡ strike [straik] v. (struck–struck/stricken) (세게) 치다, 부딪치다; (갑자기) 공격하다;
n. 공격; 치기, 때리기
If you strike someone or something, you deliberately hit them.

복습 crash [kræʃ] n. 요란한 소리; (자동차·항공기) 사고; v. 충돌하다; 박살나다; 굉음을 내다
A crash is a sudden, loud noise.

‡‡ aim [eim] v. 겨누다; 목표하다; n. 겨냥, 조준; 목적
If you aim a weapon or object at something or someone, you point it
toward them before firing or throwing it.

flick [flik] v. 탁 누르다; 잽싸게 움직이다; n. 재빨리 움직임
If you flick a switch, or flick an electrical appliance on or off, you press
the switch sharply so that it moves into a different position and works
the equipment.

‡ conduct [kándʌkt] v. 지휘하다; (특정한 활동을) 하다; n. 행동
When someone conducts an orchestra or choir, they stand in front of it
and direct its performance.

‡ orchestra [ɔ́ːrkəstrə] n. 오케스트라, 관현악단
An orchestra is a large group of musicians who play a variety of different
instruments together.

‡ signal [sígnəl] v. (동작·소리로) 신호를 보내다; 암시하다; n. 신호; 징조
If you signal to someone, you make a gesture or sound in order to send
them a particular message.

복습 flash [flæʃ] v. (잠깐) 번쩍이다; (눈 등이) 번득이다; 휙 움직이다; n. 번쩍임; 순간
If a light flashes or if you flash a light, it shines with a sudden bright light,
especially as quick, regular flashes of light.

‡ splash [splæʃ] n. 첨벙 하는 소리; v. (물 등을) 끼얹다; (액체가) 후두둑 떨어지다
A splash is the sound made when something hits water or falls into it.

be hard put to idiom (~하느라고) 애를 먹다; 어려움을 겪다
If someone is hard put to do something, they have great difficulty doing
it.

‡ **twist** [twist] v. (고개·몸 등을) 돌리다; 휘다, 구부리다; n. (손으로) 돌리기
If you twist part of your body such as your head or your shoulders, you turn that part while keeping the rest of your body still.

flicker [flíkər] v. (불·빛 등이) 깜박거리다; 움직거리다; n. (빛의) 깜박거림; 움직거림
If a light or flame flickers, it shines unsteadily.

* **pound** [paund] v. (여러 차례) 치다, 두드리다; 쿵쾅거리며 걷다
If you pound something or pound on it, you hit it with great force, usually loudly and repeatedly.

‡ **bear** [bɛər] v. 참다, 견디다; (책임 등을) 떠맡다; n. [동물] 곰
If you can't bear someone or something, you dislike them very much.

* **tap** [tæp] v. (가볍게) 톡톡 두드리다; 이용하다; n. (가볍게) 두드리기
If you tap something, you hit it with a quick light blow or a series of quick light blows.

‡ **cheek** [ʧiːk] n. 뺨, 볼; 엉덩이
Your cheeks are the sides of your face below your eyes.

tingle [tiŋgl] n. 따끔거림, 얼얼함; 흥분; v. 따끔거리다, 얼얼하다
(tingly a. 따끔거리는, 얼얼한)
If something makes your body feel tingly, it gives you a slight stinging feeling.

switch on idiom (전등 등의) 스위치를 켜다
If you switch on something like an electrical device, a machine or an engine, you start it working by pressing a switch or a button.

* **outline** [áutlàin] n. 윤곽; v. 윤곽을 보여주다
The outline of something is its general shape, especially when it cannot be clearly seen.

hazy [héizi] a. 흐릿한; 모호한; 확신이 없는
If things seem hazy, you cannot see things clearly, for example because you are feeling ill.

next door [nekst dɔ́ːr] ad. 옆 집에; n. 옆집 사람
If a room or building is next door, it is the next one to the right or left.

fill [fil] v. (구멍·틈을) 때우다; (가득) 채우다; (일·역할 등을) 하다; 충족시키다
If you fill a crack or hole, you put a substance into it in order to make the surface smooth again.

catch oneself idiom 하던 말을 멈추다
If you catch yourself saying or doing something, you suddenly keep yourself from saying or doing it.

celebrate [séləbrèit] v. 기념하다, 축하하다
If you celebrate, you do something enjoyable because of a special occasion.

occasion [əkéiʒən] n. 때, 기회; (특별한) 행사
An occasion is a time when something happens, or a case of it happening.

clever [klévər] a. 기발한, 재치 있는; 영리한, 똑똑한 (cleverness n. 재치)
A clever idea, book, or invention is extremely effective and shows the skill of the people involved.

acknowledge [æknálidʒ] v. 인정하다; 알은 척하다, 안다는 표시를 보이다
If someone's achievements, status, or qualities are acknowledged, they are known about and recognized by a lot of people, or by a particular group of people.

rely [rilái] v. 의지하다; 신뢰하다
If you rely on someone or something, you need them and depend on them in order to live or work properly.

think twice idiom 신중히 생각하다, 재고하다
If you think twice, you think carefully before you decide to do something.

tuck [tʌk] v. 단단히 덮어 주다; 집어 넣다, 끼워 넣다; n. 주름, 단
(tuck into idiom ~에게 이불을 잘 덮어 주다)
If you tuck in someone, especially a child, you cover them comfortably in bed by pulling the covers around them.

프롤로그

스탠리 램찹(Stanley Lambchop)은 자기 침대 위 어둠에 말했습니다. "난 잘 수가 없어. 내가 생각하기에는, 비가 와서 그런 것 같아."

방 건너편에 있는 침대에서는 아무 대답도 없었습니다.

"또, 난 배고파." 스탠리가 말했습니다. "너 깨어 있니, 아서(Arthur)?"

"지금은 그렇지." 그의 남동생이 말했습니다. "형이 날 깨웠잖아."

스탠리는 부엌에서 사과 하나를 가져왔고 그것을 침실 창가 근처에서 먹었습니다. 비가 더 거세졌습니다.

"난 아직도 배고파." 그가 말했습니다.

"건포도 . . . 선반에 . . ." 아서가 다시 반쯤 잠들어서, 중얼거렸습니다.

쾅! 천둥이 쳤습니다. 번개가 번쩍였습니다.

스탠리는 창문 옆 선반 위에 있는 건포도가 든 작은 상자를 찾았습니다. 그는 하나를 먹었습니다.

쾅! 번쩍!

스탠리는 건포도를 좀 더 먹었습니다.

쾅! 번쩍!

아서가 하품했습니다. "이제 자러 가. 형이 여전히 배고플 리가 없어."

"사실, 배고프진 않아." 스탠리가 침대 안으로 다시 들어갔습니다. "그런데 나는 조금 . . . 오, 달라진 것 같은 기분이야."

그는 잠이 들었습니다.

1장 스탠리는 어디에 있을까?

"아침 식사가 준비되었어요, 조지(George). 우리 아이들을 깨워야겠어요." 램찹 부인(Mrs. Lambchop)이 그녀의 남편에게 말했습니다.

바로 그때, 그가 자신의 형과 함께 쓰는 침실에서 아서 램찹이 외쳤습니다.

"이런! 이리 와보세요! 여기요!"

램찹 부부는 미소 지으면서, 이렇게 시작되었던 다른 아침을 떠올렸습니다. 그들이 발견하기로는, 거대한 게시판이, 밤사이에 스탠리 위로 떨어졌고, 그를 다치게 하지는 않았지만 반 인치(1.27센티미터)도 채 되지 않는 두께로 만들어버렸습니다. 그리고 그는 몇 주가 지난 뒤, 아서가 자전거 공기 주입 펌프로 그를 불어서 다시 둥그렇게 만들어 줄 때까지, 그 상태로 있었습니다.

"있잖아요!" 그 외침이 다시 들렸습니다. "오고 계신 거예요? 저기요(hey)!"

램찹 부인은 좋은 태도와 올바른 어법에 대해 단호한 관점을 지니고 있었습니다. "건초(hay)는 말을 위한 거지, 사람을 위한 게 아니란다, 아서." 그녀가 말하면서 그들은 침실로 들어섰습니다. "너도 잘 알다시피 말이야."

"죄송해요." 아서가 말했습니다. "문제는 말이에요, 제가 스탠리 형의 목소리는 들을 수 있는데, 형을 찾을 수가 없어요!"

램찹 부부는 방안을 둘러보았습니다. 스탠리의 침대에 있는 이불 아래에서 형태가 보였고, 베개는 마치 머리가 그 위에 놓인 것처럼 눌려 있었습니다. 하지만 머리는 없었습니다.

"왜 쳐다보시는 거예요?" 목소리는 스탠리의 것이었습니다.

미소 지으며, 램찹 씨(Mr. Lambchop)는 침대 아래를 살펴보았지만 단지 실내화 한 켤레와 낡은 테니스공만을 보았습니다. "여기에도 없어." 그가 말했습니다.

아서가 손을 뻗어서, 더듬었습니다. "아얏!" 스탠리의 목소리가 말했습니다. "네가 내 코를 찔렀어!"

아서가 헉 하고 숨을 뱉었습니다.

램찹 부인이 앞으로 나섰습니다. "내가 해보면 . . . ?" 조심스럽게, 두 손을 사용해서, 그녀가 만져보았습니다.

낄낄거리는 웃음이 침대에서 나왔습니다. "그건 간지러워요!"

"오, 이런!" 램찹 부인이 말했습니다.

그들이 과거에 일어난 정말 놀라웠던 일들을 겪으면서 그랬던 것처럼, 그녀는 램찹 씨를 보았고 그는 그녀를 보았습니다. 스탠리가 납작해진 일은 이런 일들의 시작이었습니다. 다른 일은 스탠리와 아서가 램프에서 실수로 불러낸, 하라즈 왕자(Prince Haraz)라는 어린 요정이, 그들과 함께 침실에 있는 것을 발견했던 저녁에 일어났습니다.

램찹 부인이 깊은숨을 들이마셨습니다. "우리는 사실을 직면해야만 하겠어요, 조지. 스탠리는 이제 눈에 보이지 않아요."

"엄마 말씀이 맞아요!" 깜짝 놀란 목소리가 침대에서 나왔습니다. "전 제 발을 볼 수가 없어요! 제 잠옷도요!"

"내가 이제까지 본 가장 놀라운 일이야." 램찹 씨가 말했습니다. "아니면 보지 못 한 일이라고, 난 말해야겠지. 다른 잠옷을 입어보렴, 스탠리."

스탠리가 침대에서 일어나서 다른 잠옷을 입어보았지만, 이것들도 역시 사라졌다가, 그가 그것들을 벗었을 때만 다시 나타났습니다. 그가 다음에 입어본 셔츠와 바지에도 같은 일이 일어났습니다.

"맙소사!" 램찹 부인이 자신의 고개를 저었습니다. "네가 어디에 있는지를 우리가 어떻게 알겠니, 얘야?"

"제가 알아요!" 아서가 말했습니다.

그의 침대 위에서 둥둥 떠 있던, 파티

에서 나눠준 선물인, 작은 빨간 풍선을 풀어, 그는 그 줄을 잡으라고 스탠리에게 주었습니다. "이렇게 해 봐." 그가 말했습니다.

끈은 사라졌지만, 풍선은 사라지지 않았습니다.

"됐어!" 램찹 부인이 말했습니다. "적어도 우리는 대충 말할 수 있겠구나, 스탠리가 어디에 있는지 말이야. 이제 모두 아침 식사를 하도록 해요. 그러고 나서, 조지, 우리는 댄 선생님(Dr. Dan)을 만나 이 일에 대해 뭐라고 생각하는지 들어봐야겠어요."

2장 댄 의사 선생님

"여기에서 빨간 풍선이 뭘 하는 거야?" 댄 선생님이 물었습니다. "뭐, 신경 쓰지 말자고. 안녕하세요, 램찹 부부. 스탠리와 관련된 어떤 일이 있다고, 제 간호사가 말하더군요. 그가 다시 납작해진 건 아니겠지요?"

"아니, 아니에요." 램찹 부인이 말했습니다. "그는 계속 둥근 형태를 유지하고 있어요."

"그들 대부분이 그렇죠." 댄 선생님이 말했습니다. "흠, 어린 친구를 안으로 들어오게 하지요."

"전 들어와 있어요." 스탠리가 그의

바로 앞에 서서, 말했습니다. "풍선을 들고 있어요."

"하, 하, 램찹 씨!" 댄 선생님이 말했습니다. "당신은 훌륭한 복화술사로군요! 하지만 전 당신의 작은 장난을 다 꿰뚫어 봤습니다!"

"당신이 꿰뚫어 보는 것은." 램찹 씨가 말했습니다. "바로 스탠리예요."

"뭐라고요?" 댄 선생님이 말했습니다.

"스탠리가 밤사이에 눈에 보이지 않게 되었어요." 램찹 부인이 설명했습니다. "우리는 상당히 그 일에 불안해하고 있답니다."

"두통이 있니?" 댄 선생님이 스탠리의 풍선에 물었습니다. "목이 따갑니? 배가 아프지는 않고?"

"전 괜찮아요." 스탠리가 말했습니다.

"알겠구나. 흠. . ." 댄 선생님이 자신의 고개를 저었습니다. "솔직히 말하자면, 제 오랜 경력에도 불구하고, 전 이전에 이런 일을 겪어본 적이 없습니다. 하지만 제 훌륭한 의학 서적 가운데 하나인, 프란츠 게마이스터 박사(Dr. Franz Gemeister)가 쓴 어렵고 특이한 사례들이란 책이, 도움이 될지도 모릅니다."

그는 큰 책을 그의 뒤에 있는 책꽂이에서 꺼냈고 그것을 살펴보았습니다.

"아! '보이지 않는 경우,' 134쪽." 그

가 그 책장을 찾았습니다. "흠 . . . 여기에 별 내용이 없군요, 유감스럽지만. 프랑스, 1851년: 풀랑크 부인(Madame Poulenc)이 비가 올 때 바나나를 먹다가 사라짐. 스페인, 1923년: 11살의, 곤잘레스(Gonzales) 쌍둥이가 과일 샐러드를 먹은 후에 눈에 보이지 않게 됨. 번개가 치는 것이 목격되었음. 가장 최근의 사례로는, 1968년에, 에스키모(Eskimo) 추장인 움박(Oombok)이 눈보라 속에서 통조림 복숭아를 먹는 모습이 마지막으로 목격되었음."

댄 선생님은 책을 다시 책꽂이로 돌려놓았습니다.

"그게 전부입니다." 그가 말했습니다. "게마이스터는 나쁜 날씨와 과일 사이에 어떤 관련이 있다고 의심하고 있어요."

"어젯밤에 폭풍이 쳤어요." 스탠리가 말했습니다. "그리고 전 사과를 먹었어요. 또, 건포도도요."

"이것 보세요." 댄 선생님이 말했습니다. "하지만 우리는 긍정적인 측면을 봐야 합니다, 램찹 씨 그리고 램찹 부인. 스탠리는 완벽히 건강하게 보여요, 눈에 보이는지 아닌지에 대한 요소만 세외한다면 말이지요. 우리는 단지 그를 잘 지켜봐야 할 것 같네요."

"말하기가 행동하는 것보다 더 쉽겠죠." 램찹 씨가 말했습니다. "왜 그의 옷도 같이 사라지는 걸까요?"

"유감스럽게도, 제 분야가 아니네요." 댄 선생님이 말했습니다. "전 섬유 전문가를 만나보라고 말하고 싶네요."

"선생님을 우리가 오래 붙잡고 있었네요." 램찹 부인이 말했습니다. "어서요, 조지, 스탠리—너 도대체 어디에 있니, 스탠리? 아! 풍선을 조금 더 높게 들고 있으렴, 얘야. 안녕히 계세요, 댄 선생님."

저녁 식사 시간이 되자 램찹 부부와 아서는 몹시 슬퍼졌습니다. 빨간 풍선이, 비록 스탠리가 어디에 있는지를 파악하는 데는 유용했지만, 그들에게 자신들이 얼마나 그의 사랑스러운 얼굴과 미소를 그리워하고 있는지를 계속 상기시켰습니다.

하지만 저녁을 먹은 뒤 예술적으로 재능이 있는, 램찹 부인이 빨간 풍선을 예쁜 하얀 풍선으로 바꾸었고 그녀의 수채화 물감을 꺼냈습니다. 네 가지 색상을 사용하고 여러 번의 섬세한 붓질을 해서, 그녀는 웃고 있는 스탠리의 모습을 담은 훌륭한 초상화를 하얀 풍선 위에 그렸습니다.

모두 즉시 더 쾌활해졌습니다. 스탠리는 그가 거의 예전의 자신이 된 것처럼 느껴진다고 말했습니다, 특히 그가 거울을 들여다볼 때 말이에요.

3장 첫날

다음 날 아침 램찹 부인은 스탠리의 선생님에게 쪽지를 썼고, 그의 풍선에 더 튼튼한 줄을 묶었고, 그를 학교로 보냈습니다.

"벤츨리 선생님(Miss Benchley)께." 쪽지에는 이렇게 쓰여 있었습니다. "스탠리가 예상치 못하게 눈에 보이지 않게 되었습니다. 선생님은 그가 있는지를 확인하는 데 풍선을 유용한 지침으로 삼으면 될 것입니다. 해리엇 램찹(Harriet Lambchop) 올림."

벤츨리 선생님이 학급에 말했습니다. "우리는 스탠리가 있으리라고 여겨지는 곳을 쳐다보면 안 됩니다." 그녀가 말했습니다. "또는 그의 상태에 대해서 험담을 해서도 안 됩니다."

그럼에도, 소문은 곧 신문에까지 퍼졌습니다. 기자가 학교를 찾아왔고 그의 이야기가 다음 날 실렸습니다.

표제는 이렇게 쓰였습니다: 미소 짓는 학생: "당신이 그를 본 적이 있다면, 이제는 그럴 수가 없습니다!" 그 아래에는 두 사진이 있었는데, 이전의 것과 이후의 것이었습니다.

그 이전 사진은, 그 전주에 벤츨리 선생님이 찍은 것으로, 자신의 책상에 앉은 미소 짓는 스탠리의 모습을 보여주었습니다. 이후 사진은, 기자가 찍은 것으로, 단지 스탠리의 책상과 그의 웃는 얼굴이 담긴 풍선이 그 위에서 까딱거리고 있는 모습만을 보여주었습니다. 그 기사에는 스탠리가 정말 자기 책상에 있으며, 그녀가 아는 한, 웃고 있다고 말한 벤츨리 선생님의 발언이 포함되었습니다.

램찹 부부는 다른 지역에 사는 친구들을 위해 여러 부수의 신문을 샀습니다. 램찹 부인이 말하기를, 자신의 화려한 풍선 예술 작품이 흑백 사진에서 그 빛을 잃었지만, 전반적으로 잘 나온 사진이라고 했습니다.

아서는 "보이지 않는 소년의 동생"도 재미있는 사진이 되었을 것이라며, 기자가 다시 방문한다면, 스탠리가 그걸 제안해야 한다고 말했습니다.

* * *

눈에 보이지 않는 게 유혹이 될 수도 있다고, 램찹 부부가 경고하면서, 그렇지만 스탠리가 그 유혹을 이겨내야 한다고 했습니다. 예를 들어, 사람들을 염탐하거나, 그들이 뭐라고 말하는지 들으려고 사람들에게 몰래 다가가는 일을 하는 것은 옳지 않다고 했습니다.

하지만 다음 주 토요일 오후에, 램찹 가족이 극장에 갔을 때, 이를 이겨내지 못하는 사람은 바로 아서였습니다.

"스탠리 형을 위한 좌석 표를 사지 말아요." 그가 매표소에서 속삭였습니다. "그냥 형의 풍선을 숨기면 되잖아요. 누가 알겠어요?"

"그건 기만하는 행동이란다, 얘야." 램찹 부인이 말했습니다. "좌석 네 개, 부탁해요," 그녀가 매표소에 있는 여자에게 말했습니다. "우리는 우리 코트를 놓을 자리를 원하거든요, 당신도 알겠지만."

"그건 일종의, 기만하는 행동이 아니에요?" 그들이 안으로 들어설 때 아서가 물었습니다.

"같은 방식으로는 아니지." 램찹 씨가 말하면서, 자기 좌석 아래로 스탠리의 풍선을 집어넣었습니다.

영화가 시작되자마자, 매우 키가 큰 남자가 스탠리의 바로 앞에 앉아, 그의 시야를 가렸습니다. 램찹 씨는 스탠리를 자신의 무릎 위에 앉혔는데, 그곳에서 화면이 수월하게 보였고, 훨씬 더 뒤에 앉은 사람들도 그 사실을 알지 못한 채 그를 곧장 꿰뚫어보았습니다. 스탠리는 그 영화를 몹시 즐겼습니다.

"봤죠?" 그들이 밖으로 나갈 때 아서가 말했습니다. "스탠리 형은 심지어 자리가 필요하지 않았어요."

"네 말도 일리가 있구나." 다리가 저린, 램찹 씨가 말했습니다.

4장 공원에서 일어난 일

일요일 오후였습니다. 아서는 친구를 만나러 나갔기에, 램찹 부부는 스탠리와 함께 가까운 공원으로 갔습니다. 거리는 북적였고, 스탠리는 바쁘게 지나가는 사람들에게 거칠게 떠밀리는 위험을 줄이기 위해서 자신의 풍선을 들고 있었습니다.

공원 근처에서 그들은 램찹 씨의 오래된 대학 친구인 랠프 존스(Ralph Johnes)를 만났습니다.

"자네 가족을 만나는 것은 항상 즐거운 일이야, 조지!" 존스 씨가 말했습니다. "큰아들이 한때는 납작했지, 내가 기억하기로는 말이야. 자네는 그를 돌돌 말아서 데리고 다녔지. 그리고 한때 외국에서 온 소년과 함께 있었지. 왕자였지, 응?"

"자네 정말 기억력이 좋군!" 램찹 씨가 말하면서, 그때 그들과 같이 있었던 어린 요정을 떠올렸습니다.

"당신은 어떻게 지내세요, 랠프?" 램찹 부인이 물었습니다. "스탠리? 존스 씨에게 인사해야지."

"안녕하시오!" 존스 씨가 말했습니다. "저 풍선은 떠 있는데—흠 . . . 근데 스탠리는 어디에 있는 건가?"

"풍선을 들고 있어요." 스탠리가 말했습니다. "전 어째서인지 눈에 보이지 않게 됐어요."

"그러니? 처음에는 납작해지고, 이제
는 보이지 않다니." 랠프 존스가 자신의
고개를 저었습니다. "아이들이란! 늘 이
래저래 바쁘지, 어, 조지? 내 첫째 애가
치과 진료를 받아야 해. 뭐, 난 가야 할
것 같군! 왕자에게 내 안부를 전해줘.
파우지 무스타파 아슬란 미르자 멜렉
나머드 하라즈 왕자였지, 내 기억엔."

"정말로 뛰어난 기억이네요." 램찹 부
인이 말하는 동안 존스 씨는 떠났습니
다.

공원에 있는 들판 주위에서, 램찹 가족
은 벤치를 찾아 그곳에 앉아 쉬었습니
다.

들판 위에서는, 아이들이 자전거를
타고 경주를 하며, 빙글빙글 돌고 있었
습니다. 갑자기, 고함이 났습니다. "포기
해, 빌리(Billy)! . . . 빌리는 잘 못하잖
아! . . . 빌리, 빌리, 바보 같은 빌리, 그
는 자전거도 탈 줄 모른대요!"

"저 애가 분명 빌리일 거예요." 램찹
부인이 말했습니다. "다른 아이들보다
한참 뒤처져 있는 작은 녀석 말이에요.
오, 맙소사! 그가 얼마나 비틀거리는지
좀 봐요!"

스탠리는 자신이 자전거를 타는 것
을 배우고 있을 때 그가 얼마나 긴장했
었는지 그리고 어떻게 자신의 아버지가

그를 흔들리지 않게 잡아주었는지 기억
했습니다. 불쌍한 빌리! 만약 그럴 수만
있다면 . . . 내가 그럴 수 있어! 그는 생
각했고, 벤치에 자신의 풍선을 묶었습니
다.

빌리가 다시 돌아서 왔을 때, 스탠리
를 빠르게 들판으로 뛰어갔습니다. 비
틀거리는 자전거를 뒤에 붙잡고, 그는
달리기 시작했습니다.

"오–이런!" 속도가 붙는 것에 깜짝 놀
라면서, 빌리는 말했습니다.

스탠리는 더 열심히 달리면서, 계속
자전거가 흔들리지 않게 했습니다. 페
달이 점점 더 빨리 올라갔다가 내려갔
고, 여전히 더 빨리 돌아갔습니다.

"이크!" 빌리가 외쳤습니다.

스탠리는 자신이 할 수 있는 한 최대
한 빨리 달렸습니다. 곧 그들은 바로 앞
에 있는 남자아이를 지나쳤고, 다음에
는 다른 남자아이를 또 다른 아이를 지
나쳤습니다! 그들이 다른 모든 아이들
을 지나치고 나서야 스탠리는, 이제 숨
이 차서, 자전거를 놓았습니다.

"휘이이이이!" 빌리가 외쳤고 다시 한
번 스스로 한 바퀴를 달렸습니다.

"네가 이겼어, 빌리!" 다른 남자아이
들이 소리쳤습니다. "어떻게 그렇게 잘
타게 된 거야? . . . 그리고 그렇게 갑
자기! . . . 너는 분명히 우리를 속인 거
야!"

스탠리는 자신의 호흡을 되찾았고 벤치에 앉은 램찹 부부에게로 돌아왔습니다.

"네가 그걸 놓쳐서 너무 안 됐구나, 스탠리." 자신이 진실을 알지 못하는 것처럼 굴면서, 램찹 씨가 말했습니다. "저 비틀거리던 작은 남자아이가—그가 갑자기 매우 잘 타게 되었단다."

"오?" 스탠리도 역시 모르는 척하면서, 말했습니다. "제가 관심을 기울이지 않고 있었나 봐요."

램찹 씨가 그의 가슴을 살짝 쿡 하고 찔렀습니다.

30분 정도가 흘렀고, 램찹 부인은 그들이 햇볕 아래 너무 오래 앉아있는지도 모른다고 걱정했습니다. 스탠리의 현재 상태에서는, 그녀가 말하기로는, 햇볕에 심하게 탔는지 알아차리기 어려울 것이라고 했습니다.

바로 그때, 젊은 남자와 예쁜 여자가 손을 잡은 채, 천천히 걸어가며 지나갔고, 가까이에 있는 작은 나무숲에서 멈췄습니다.

"저 사람은 내 친한 친구인 호지슨 부인(Mrs. Hodgson)의 아들, 필립(Phillip)이에요." 램찹 부인이 말했습니다. "그리고 저 여자는 분명 그의 여자친구, 루시아(Lucia)일 거예요. 정말 슬픈 이야기에요! 그들은 사랑하고 있고

필립은 정말 결혼해달라고 청혼하고 싶어 하지요. 하지만 그는 너무 부끄러움이 많아요. 호지슨 부인이 말하기로는, 그가 시도하고 또 시도하지만, 매번 그의 용기가 꺾인다고 하네요. 그리고 루시아는 너무 소심해서 그에게서 청혼을 끌어낼 수 없고요."

램찹 씨는 조금도 부끄러워하지 않는 사람이었습니다. "내가 가서 내 소개를 해야겠어요." 그가 말했습니다. "그리고 그를 대신해서 청혼을 하지요."

"안 돼요, 조지." 램찹 부인이 자신의 고개를 흔들었습니다. "루시아는 반드시 그 말을 필립의 입으로 직접 들어야 해요."

스탠리에게 아이디어가 떠올랐습니다.

"금방 다녀올게요!" 그가 말했고, 젊은 커플이 서 있는 나무숲으로 달려갔습니다. 그들 곁에 도착하자마자, 그는 매우 가만히 서 있었습니다.

". . . 좋은 날씨야, 루시아, 그렇게 생각하지 않아?" 필립이 말하고 있었습니다. "하지만 비가 올 수도 있다고 하더라고. 누가 알겠어?"

"난 분명히 네 말이 꽤 옳다고 생각해, 필립." 그 여자가 대답했습니다. "난 날씨에 대한 네 의견을 정말 높이 사고 있어."

"넌 상냥해, 정말 친절하지." 필립이

약간 떨었습니다. "루시아, 내가 묻고 싶은 게 있는데 . . . 내 말은 . . . 너 있잖아 . . . 동의하니, 그게 있지 . . ." 그가 침을 꿀꺽 삼켰습니다. "네가 입은 드레스가 정말 예쁘네!"

"고마워." 루시아가 말했습니다. "난 네 넥타이가 맘에 들어. 네가 뭐라고 말하고 있었지, 필립?"

"아!" 필립이 말했습니다. "맞아! 그래! 얼마 전부터, 사랑하는 루시아 . . . 내 간절한 소망은 . . . 오, 이런! 나는 원하는데 . . ." 그가 자신의 입술을 깨물었습니다. "봐! 먹구름이야, 저기 서쪽에 말이야! 결국 비가 오겠는걸."

"그러지 않으면 좋겠어." 루시아는 거의 울 것처럼 보였습니다. "내 말은, 비가 오게 되면 . . . 뭐, 우리가 젖게 되잖아."

이건 몹시 지루하네, 스탠리가 생각했습니다.

대화는 훨씬 더 지루해져만 갔습니다. 다시 그리고 또다시 필립은 자신의 사랑을 알리는 데 실패하고, 대신 날씨나, 나무의 모양, 또는 공원에서 노는 아이들에 대해 수다를 떨었습니다.

"난 묻고 싶은데, 사랑하는 루시아." 필립이 아마도 스무 번째 묻기 시작했습니다, "만약에 네가 . . . 그게 있지 . . . 만약 네가 . . . 만약에 . . ."

"응?" 루시아도 역시 스무 번째로 말

했습니다. "뭐야, 필립? 넌 무엇을 말하고 싶은 거야?"

스탠리가 앞으로 몸을 기울였습니다.

"루시아 . . . ?" 필립이 말했습니다. "흠 . . . 아! 난 . . ."

"나와 결혼해 줘!" 스탠리가 자신의 목소리를 가능한 필립의 것과 비슷하게 흉내 내며, 말했습니다.

루시아의 두 눈이 휘둥그레졌습니다. "그럴게, 필립!" 그녀가 외쳤습니다. "물론 난 너와 결혼할 거야!"

필립이 마치 그가 기절할 것처럼 보였습니다. "뭐? 내가 했나—? 그럴 거라고?"

루시아가 그를 안아주었고, 그들은 키스했습니다.

"내가 마침내 청혼하다니!" 필립이 외쳤습니다. "난 내가 그 말을 했다는 걸 거의 믿을 수가 없어!"

당신이 하지는 않았지, 스탠리는 생각했습니다.

램찹 부부는 그 연인이 포옹하는 것을 보았습니다. "잘했어, 스탠리!" 그가 그들이 있는 벤치로 돌아왔을 때 그들이 말했고, 집에 가는 길에도 몇 번이나 말했습니다.

호지슨 부인은 그날 저녁 필립과 루시아가 곧 결혼할 것이라고 알리려고 전화했습니다. 정말 멋진 일이야! 램찹 부인이 말했습니다. 그녀는 바로 그날 오후에 그들이 공원에 있는 것을 보았습니다. 정말 잘 어울리는 한 쌍이야! 서로 정말 사랑하고!

스탠리가 엄마를 놀렸습니다. "엄마는 절대로 사람들에게 몰래 다가가거나 그들을 염탐하면 안 된다고 하셨잖아요. 하지만 전 오늘 그랬지요. 엄마 저한테 화나셨어요?"

"오, 매우 화났지." 램찹 부인이 말했고, 그의 머리 위에 키스해 주었습니다.

5장 TV 프로그램

아서는 따돌림받는 기분이 들었습니다. "스탠리 형은 항상 재미있는 모험을 하고는 해요." 그가 말했습니다. "그리고 그 신문 기사도 단지 형에 대한 것만 실렸죠. 아무도 저한테는 관심이 없어요."

"관심을 끄는 가장 좋은 방법은, 얘야." 램찹 부인이 말했습니다. "그 사람의 성격을 통해서란다. 친절하게 굴고. 그리고 공평하게. 명랑함도 무척 칭찬받는단다, 재치도 마찬가지고."

"전 그 모든 걸 다 할 수는 없어요." 아서가 말했습니다.

램찹 부인은 스탠리에게 은밀하게 이야기했습니다. "네 동생이 조금 시샘하는 것 같구나." 그녀가 말했습니다.

"제가 납작했을 때, 아서는 사람들이 절 쳐다봐서 시샘했어요." 스탠리가 말했습니다. "이제는 그들이 저를 전혀 볼 수 없고, 걔는 또 질투하잖아요."

램찹 부인이 한숨 쉬었습니다. "만약 네가 그를 기운 나게 할 방법을 찾는다면, 그렇게 하렴."

바로 다음 날 중요한 방송국 사람이 램찹 씨에게 전화했습니다.

"전 테디 토커(Teddy Talker)입니다, 램찹 씨." 그가 말했습니다. "엄청 유명한 TV 프로그램, 테디 토커와의 이야기 (Talking with Teddy Talker)의 사회자입니다. 스탠리가 거기에 나올 수 있나요?"

"스탠리가 어디에라도 나타난다면 우린 기쁘겠지요." 램찹 씨가 말했습니다. "사람들은 그를 볼 수 없어요, 당신도 알다시피."

"제가 그냥 그가 거기에 있다고 말하면 됩니다." 테디 토커가 말했습니다. "그 아이와 말해 보세요. 그리고 저한테 알려주세요."

스탠리는 자신이 TV에 출연하는 것을 특별히 신경 쓰지 않는다고 했습니다. 하지만 그때 그는 아서를 기운 나게 하는 것에 대해 기억했습니다.

"좋아요." 그가 말했습니다. "하지만 아서도, 나가야 해요. 그는 재미있는 이야기를 하는 것과 마술 묘기를 부리는 것을 좋아하잖아요. 우리 둘 다 프로그램에 나갈 거라고 말해주세요."

아서는 매우 기뻤고, 그날 저녁에 형제는 자신들이 무엇을 할지 계획을 세웠습니다. 다음 날 아침 램찹 씨가 테디 토커에게 말했습니다.

"좋은 계획이에요!" 방송국 사람이 말했습니다. "이번 주 금요일, 어때요? 고마워요, 램찹!"

"모두, 환영합니다!" 테디 토커가 자기 TV 프로그램의 무대에서 금요일 저녁에 말했습니다. "오늘 밤은 멋진 게스트들이 왔습니다! 보이지 않는 소년을 포함해서 말이에요!"

앞줄에는, 나머지 관객과 함께 손뼉을 치는, 램찹 부부가 지금은 무대 뒤편에 있는 분장실에서 기다리는 스탠리와 아서를 생각했습니다. 그들이 얼마나 신이 났을까!

다른 게스트들은 이미 테디 토커의 책상 옆에 있는 소파에 앉아있었습니다. 그는 처음에는 소시지에 대한 책을 쓴 여자와, 다음에는 랍비(rabbi)가 된 테니스 챔피언, 그리고는 미인 대회에서 우승했지만, 지금은 세계 평화에 기여하기 위해 헌신할 계획을 세운 매우 아름다운 젊은 여자와 대화를 나누었습니다.

마침내 램찹의 계획을 시작하는 안내 문구가 나왔습니다.

"보이지 않는 스탠리가 늦어지고 있지만 여기게 곧 도착할 것입니다." 테디 토커가 관객에게 말했습니다. "그동안에, 우리는 다행히도 그의 매우 재능이 있는 동생과 함께할 것입니다!"

항의가 빗발쳤습니다. "동생이라고? . . . 눈에 보이는 동생? . . . 젠장! . . . 우리가 공짜로 들어와서 다행이군!"

"신사 숙녀 여러분!" 테디 토커가 말했습니다. "아서 램찹과 함께하는 즐거운 마술 쇼입니다!"

아서가 무대 위로 나갔는데, 램찹 부인이 그를 위해 만들어준 깔끔한 검은색 마술사 망토를 걸치고 있었고 작은 상자를 들고 있었는데, 이를 테디 토커의 책상 위에 올려놨습니다.

"안녕하세요, 여러분!" 그가 말했습니다. "상자는 다음에 할 쇼를 위한 것입니다. 지금은 즐겁게 놀아 봐요! 땅에 있는 세 개의 구멍에 대한 이야기를 들어본 적 있나요?" 그는 미소 지으며, 기다렸습니다. "Well, well, well!"

두 사람은 웃었지만, 그게 전부였습니다.

"난 이해하지 못 하겠어요." 램찹 부부의 뒤에 앉은 여자가 말했습니다.

램찹 씨가 자신의 자리에서 돌아앉았습니다. "'well(우물)'은 땅에 난 구멍이지요." 그가 말했습니다. "'Well, well,

well,' 세 개의 구멍이 되는 셈이에요."

"아! 알겠어요!" 여자가 말했습니다.

"수수께끼입니다, 신사 숙녀 여러분!" 아서가 외쳤습니다. "왕들이 그들의 군대(armies)를 어디에 둘까요?"

"어디인가요?" 누군가 외쳤습니다.

"그들의 sleevies입니다!" 아서가 말했습니다.

이번에는 첫 번째 농담을 이해하지 못 했던 그 여자를 포함한, 많은 사람이 웃었습니다. "저건 이해했어요," 그녀가 말했습니다.

"독심술 묘기입니다!" 아서가 선언했습니다. 그는 카드 한 벌을 섞었고 테디 토커에게 한 장을 뽑게 했습니다.

"제가 그걸 보지 못 하게 하세요!" 그가 말했습니다. "하지만 그걸 보세요! 당신의 마음속에 그걸 그려 보세요! 전 집중하며, 제 마술의 힘을 이용할 것입니다!" 아서가 자신의 눈을 감았습니다. "흠 . . . 흠 . . . 당신의 카드는요, 선생님, 하트 4입니다!"

"맞아요!" 테디 토커가 외쳤습니다. "그건 정말 하트 4예요!"

목소리가 다시 높아졌습니다. "훌륭해! . . . 그가 마음을 읽을 수 있다고? . . . 저렇게 어린데도! . . . 한 번 더 해 보렴, 얘야!"

"물론이죠!" 아서가 말했습니다.

하지만 그는 모든 카드가 하트 4였던 가짜 카드 한 벌을 사용했었고, 만약 그 카드의 이름이 다시 불린다면 관객은 분명 그 사실을 눈치챌 것입니다. 다행스럽게도, 형제는 이에 대해 생각해 두었습니다. 무대 뒤에서, 스탠리가 자신의 풍선을 한 의자에 묶었습니다.

아서는 이제 진짜 카드 한 벌을 섞었고, 지원자가 필요하다고 했습니다. 한 나이든 신사가 무대 위로 올라왔을 때, 스탠리는 발끝으로 살금살금 걸어 나가 그의 뒤에 섰습니다. 관객은 그 지원자에게 박수를 보냈습니다. 이건 정말 이상한 일이지 뭐야! 스탠리는 생각했습니다. 수백 명의 사람들이 보고 있지만, 어느 한 사람도 나를 보지 못하다니!

"카드 한 장을 뽑으세요, 선생님!" 아서가 말했습니다. "고맙습니다! 그것을 잘 감춰두세요! 하지만 그걸 마음속에 그려보세요!" 다시 자신의 눈을 감고서, 그는 열심히 생각하는 척했습니다.

재빨리 살펴보자 스탠리는 지원자가 클럽 10을 쥐고 있다는 것을 알았습니다. 그는 살금살금 걸어가서 자기 동생의 귀에 대고 속삭였습니다.

아서가 자신의 눈을 떴습니다. "제가 알아냈어요. 카드는 . . . 클럽 10입니다!"

"맞아요! 훌륭해요!" 나이든 신사가 소리쳤습니다. 관객은 그가 자기 자리로 돌아가는 동안 열렬히 박수를 보냈습니다.

램찹 씨는 자기 뒤에 있는 여자에게 미소 지었습니다. "우리 아들이에요." 그가 말했습니다.

"정말 재주가 좋네요!" 여자가 말했습니다. "그가 다음에는 무엇을 할까요?"

램찹 부인은 깊은숨을 들이마셨습니다. 그날 아침 스탠리와 아서는 옆집에 사는 남자아이에게서 애완 개구리를 빌렸습니다. 그녀는 알고 있었는데, 다음에 무엇이 오든지, 그건 이 저녁의 계획 가운데 가장 대담한 부분이 되리라는 것을요!

"신사 숙녀 여러분!" 아서가 말했습니다. "새로운 종류의 마술입니다! 아서 램찹—그게 바로 저예요!—그리고 헨리(Henry), 공중에서 춤을 추는 개구리입니다!"

그가 테디 토커의 책상 위에 있는 상자에서 헨리를 들었고 그를 위로 올렸습니다. 헨리는, 마치 미소 짓는 것처럼 보였는데, H가 쓰인 작은 하얀 셔츠를 입고 있었고, 이 역시 램찹 부인이 만든 것이었습니다.

"날아라, 헨리!" 아서가 소리쳤습니다. "훨훨 날아가서 공중에서 그대로 멈춰라!"

앞으로 나서면서, 스탠리는 아서의 손에서 헨리를 빼내어 무대의 저편으로 달려갔습니다. 거기에서 그가 멈춰서, 개구리를 자기 머리 위에 높이 들어 올렸습니다. 헨리가 그 다리를 꿈틀꿈틀 움직였습니다.

"놀라워!" 관객이 외쳤습니다. "누가 그걸 믿을 수 있겠어? . . . 저건 굉장한 개구리야! . . . 무엇이 녀석을 계속 위에 떠 있게 하는 걸까?"

"돌아 봐, 헨리!" 아서가 명령했습니다. "공중에 돌아 봐!"

스탠리가 빠르게 원을 그리며 걸으면서, 그가 가는 대로 헨리를 흔들었습니다.

관객은 굉장히 감명 받았습니다. "정말 뛰어난 마술사야! . . . 독심술 그리고 나는 개구리까지! . . . 저런 건 매일 볼 수 있는 게 아니라고!"

헨리의 비행을 통제하는 척하면서, 아서가 계속 손가락으로 가리키는 동안 스탠리는 무대를 온통 휘저으면서 개구리가 공중에서 내리 덮치게 했습니다. "이런!" 헨리가 그의 책상 위로 날아들자 테디 토커가 외쳤습니다. 긴 소파 위에서는, 소시지에 대해 쓴 작가와 테니스를 하던 랍비 그리고 미인 대회 우승자가 머리를 수그렸습니다. 심지어 램찹 부부도, 헨리의 비행에 대한 비밀을 알고 있음에도, 그것이 놀라운 광경이라고 생각했습니다.

마침내, 큰 박수를 받으면서, 아서는 헨리를 자기 손으로 거두어 그를 다시 작은 상자 안으로 돌려놓았습니다.

스탠리는 자신의 웃는 표정을 한 풍선을 가지러 살금살금 걸어 나갔습니다. 계획은 이제 테디 토커가 보이지 않는 소년이 도착했음을 알리고 그를 소개하는 것이었습니다.

하지만 아서가 다시 앞으로 나섰습니다.

"제게 환호해 주셔서 고맙습니다." 그가 관객에게 말했습니다. "하지만 전 말할 것이 있어요. 처음에 한 독심술 묘기는, 그건 제가 진짜로 한 거예요. 하지만 두 번째 묘기는 . . . 사실, 전 독심술을 전혀 할 수 없어요. 그리고 나는 개구리는, 그가―"

목소리가 커졌습니다. "독심술을 할 수 없다고?" . . . "우리는 속았던 거야?" . . . "개구리가 거짓말을 한다고?" . . . "개구리 말고, 이 멍청아!" . . . "잠깐, 그의 말이 다 끝나지 않았어!"

"제발! 들어주세요!" 아서가 말했습니다. "여러분이 제가 혼자 모든 것을 다 했다고 여기게 하는 것은 공정하지 않아요. 전 조수가 있었어요! 두 번째 묘기를 할 때, 그가 카드를 보고 제게 그게 무엇인지 말해줬습니다. 그리고 헨리는 . . . 뭐, 제 조수가 공중에서 그를 쌩 하고 지나가게 했어요!"

이쯤 되자 관객은 몹시 혼란스러워했습니다. "누군데?" . . . "무슨 조수 말이야?" . . . "그건 그냥 평범한 개구리였어?" . . . "그런데 어떤 개구리는 날기도 한다고!" . . . "아니, 다람쥐가 날지, 개구리는 아니야!" . . . "쌩 하고 지나가게 하다니?"

아서가 계속 말했습니다. "제 형, 스탠리가 저를 도와주었어요! 제가 이 프로그램에 나올 수 있도록 그가 준비해 주었어요! 그는 무척 좋은 형이에요, 그리고 전 형에게 정말 고마워요!"

테디 토커가 벌떡 일어났습니다. "신사 숙녀 여러분! 제가 이제 내내 이곳에 있었던, 아주 특별한 게스트를 소개하겠습니다! 보이지 않는 소년! 스탠리 램챱입니다!"

스탠리가 자신의 웃는 표정을 한 풍선을 가지고, 무대 위로 나왔습니다. 아서는 자신의 손을 내밀었고 관객은 스탠리가 그 손을 잡았다는 것을 알 수 있었습니다. 엄청난 박수갈채가 쏟아졌습니다.

형제는 계속해서 허리 굽혀 인사했고, 스탠리의 풍선이 위아래로 까딱거렸습니다. 아서의 미소는 분명하게 보였고, 램챱 부부는, 박수를 보내면서, 심지어 풍선에 그려진 미소도 그 전보다 더 환하게 보이는 것 같다고 생각했습니다.

"저도 두 아이가 있어요." 그들 뒤에 있는 여자가 말했습니다. "둘 다 완전히 눈에 보이고 연극적인 재능은 없지요. 우리는 아주 평범한 가족이에요."

"우리도 그렇답니다." 램찹 씨가 미소 지으며, 말했습니다. "대부분은, 그렇다는 거죠."

아서는 무대를 떠났고, 스탠리는 소시지에 대해 쓴 작가와 미인 대회 우승자 사이의 소파 위에 앉았고 테디 토커의 질문에 답했습니다. 그는 자신이 어떻게 눈에 보이지 않게 되었는지 모른다고, 말했고, 그가 종종 부딪히게 되고 사람들에게 자신이 거기에 있다는 것을 계속 상기시켜야 해서 그렇게 지내는 것이 사실은 그렇게 좋은 일만은 아니하고 했습니다. 그 이후에, 테디 토커는 모든 사람에게 와 줘서 고맙다고 했고 프로그램은 끝났습니다.

다시 집으로 돌아와서, 아서는 그날 저녁이 순조로웠다고 여겼습니다.

"전 많은 박수를 받았어요." 그가 말했습니다. "하지만 아마도 그건 대부분 스탠리 형이 한 일 때문일 거예요. 전 지나치게 자만하면 안 될 것 같아요."

"침착함과 좋은 유머 감각은 연기자의 성공에 크게 기여를 한단다." 램찹 부인이 말했습니다. "넌 그 두 가지 경우 모두 잘 해냈어. 헨리는 아침에 돌려주렴, 얘야. 이제 잘 시간이란다."

6장 은행 강도들

램찹 씨와 스탠리 그리고 아서는 TV로 저녁 뉴스를 보고 있었습니다.

". . . 내일 더 끔찍한 사건과 폭력적인 일을 전하겠습니다." 뉴스 진행자가 국내 사건들에 대한 보도를 마치면서, 말했습니다. "여기 우리의 아름다운 도시에서 이번 달에 세 번째로, 오늘 또 다른 은행에 도둑이 들었습니다. 이 독특한 강도들은—"

"범죄 이야기는 그만해요!" 서둘러 들어오면서, 램찹 부인이 TV를 껐습니다. "저녁 먹으러 와요!"

스탠리는 어떻게 그 강도들이 독특하다는 건지 절대 알지 못할 거라고 생각했습니다. 하지만 다음 날 오후, 그의 아버지와 산책하다가, 그는 알게 되었습니다. 집으로 가는 길에 그들이 은행을 지나갔습니다.

"난 수표를 현금으로 바꿔야 하는데, 저 안은 매우 붐비는구나." 램찹 씨가 말했습니다. "여기서 기다리렴, 스탠리."

스탠리는 기다렸습니다.

갑자기, 은행 안에서 고함이 들렸습니다. "여자 은행 강도다! 사람들이 TV에서 말하던 것처럼 말이야!" . . . "난 그걸 들었을 때 웃었는데!" . . . "나도 그랬어!"

한 사람은 통통하고, 다른 사람은 매

우 키가 큰, 드레스를 입고 고급 모자를 쓴 두 여자가, 각자 한 손에는 돈 가방을 그리고 다른 손에는 권총을 들고, 은행에서 도망쳐 나왔습니다.

"거기 있어!" 높고 갈라진 목소리로, 통통한 여자가 은행에 대고 외쳤습니다. "누구도 밖으로 도망치지 마! 그렇지 않으면 . . . 빵! 빵!"

"맞아!" 키 큰 여자가 역시 이상하고 높은 목소리로 소리쳤습니다. "단지 우리가 여자라고 해서 우리가 총을 쏘지 못하는 건 아니라고!"

총알이 날아다닌다면 눈에 보이지 않는 건 나를 지켜주지 못할 거야! 스탠리가 생각했습니다. 그는 숨을 곳을 찾았습니다.

빈 냠냠 아이스크림 승합차가 근처에 주차되어 있었고 그는 그 안으로 뛰어들었습니다. 문에 그 줄이 걸려서, 그의 풍선이 여전히 승합차 밖에서 떠 있었지만, 그는 감히 그것을 가져올 엄두를 내지 못했습니다. 초콜릿 냠냠, 딸기 냠냠, 그리고 바삭바삭 냠냠 이라고 적힌 판지로 된 대형 통 뒤에 몸을 웅크리고 앉아서, 그가 살짝 내다보았습니다.

경보음이 은행 안에서 울리고 있었고, 외치는 소리가 다시 났습니다. "하! 이제 당신들은 곤경에 처할 거야!" . . . "경찰이 올 거라고!" . . . "아가씨들, 그 돈을 발견한 곳에 다시 그걸 돌려놔!"

그때 스탠리는 두 여자 강도들이 돈 가방을 들고, 그를 향해서 달려오는 것을 보았습니다. 그들이 멈추고 있었습니다! 그들이 냠냠 승합차에 오르고 있었습니다!

다시 몸을 아래로 웅크리며, 그가 숨을 죽였습니다.

강도들은 이제 승합차에 탔고, 그가 숨은 곳 가까이에 있었습니다. "서둘러!" 통통한 여자가 놀랍게도 낮은 목소리로 말했습니다. "이 구두 때문에 아파 죽겠다고!"

키가 큰 여자가 바삭바삭 냠냠 통을 열었고, 스탠리는 그것이 비었다는 걸 보았습니다. 그러더니 두 강도는 그들의 가방에서 돈다발들을 통 안으로 부었고 다시 뚜껑을 위에 덮었습니다.

스탠리는 자신이 그다음에 본 것을 거의 믿을 수가 없었습니다!

강도들은 자신들의 고급 모자를 옆으로 던졌고 가발을 당겨 벗었습니다. 그리고 이제 그들은 자신들의 머리 위로 그들의 드레스를 당기며, 옷을 벗고 있었습니다!

그들은 남자였어, 스탠리가 알아차렸습니다, 여자가 아니었다고! 그래! 드레스 아래로 그들은 하얀 아이스크림을 파는 사람의 바지를 위로 돌돌 말아서 입고 있었고, 하얀 냠냠 셔츠를 입고 있었습니다!

"휴! 살 것 같아, 하워드(Howard)!" 통통한 강도가 자신의 여자 구두를 차서 벗고 하얀 운동화를 신었습니다.

"그들은 이제 우리를 절대 잡지 못 할 거야, 랠프(Ralph)!" 키 큰 강도가 말했습니다.

강도들은 자신들의 바짓가랑이를 내렸고 자신들의 여자 옷을 초콜릿 냠냠 이라고 표시된, 또 다른 빈 통에 던져 넣었습니다. 그리고는 그들은 앞좌석으로 뛰어 올라탔고, 키 큰 남자가 운전하면서, 승합차는 속도를 내며 떠났습니다.

통 뒤에서, 스탠리는 다시 숨을 죽였습니다. 이 두 사람은 붙잡히기에는 너무 똑똑했습니다! 그들은 분명 도망치게 될 것입니다! 어느 누구도 두 냠냠 아이스크림 판매원이 여자 행세를 하리라고는 의심하지 않을 것입니다— 그런데 승합차가 속도를 줄이고 있었습니다! 그것이 멈추고 있었어요!

스탠리는 다시 밖을 살짝 내다보았습니다.

경찰차가 길을 막고 두 경찰관이 그 옆에 서서, 지나가는 차량을 검문하고 있었습니다. 잠시 후 그들이 냠냠 아이스크림 승합차 옆에 왔습니다.

"은행에 도둑이 들었어요." 첫 번째 경찰관이 운전자에게 말했습니다. "두 여자한테요. 당신들 아이스크림 판매원들은 의심스럽게 보이는 여성들을 본

적 있나요?"

"맙소사!" 키 큰 남자가 자신의 고개를 저었습니다. "최근에는 갈수록, 여자들이 한때는 남자들이 했던 역할을 차지한다니까요.아이고, 맙소사!"

그의 옆에서, 통통한 남자가 서둘러 말했습니다. "하지만 은행 강도라고, 하워드, 그건 잘못된 일이야."

두 번째 경찰관이 승합차의 뒤를 살펴보았습니다. "그냥 여기에는 아이스크림만 있어." 그가 자기 파트너에게 말했습니다.

이 사기 행각이 통하고 있어! 스탠리가 생각했습니다. 내가 어떻게 하면 . . . ? 아이디어가 그에게 떠올랐습니다. 손을 뻗어서, 그가 초콜릿 냠냠 통의 뚜껑을 휙 뒤집었습니다.

"헐거운 뚜껑이네요." 두 번째 경찰관이 말했습니다. "꼭 닫는 것이 좋겠— 이봐요! 이 통은 여자 옷으로 가득하잖아요!"

"오!" 키 큰 남자가 슬픈 표정을 지었습니다. "어려운 사람을 위한 거예요." 그가 말했습니다. "그것들은 제 돌아가신 어머니의 옷이랍니다."

스탠리가 바삭바삭 냠냠 통의 뚜껑을 휙 하고 뒤집어 열었고 돈다발이 명백하게 보였습니다!

"당신의 어머니는 굉장히 부유한 여자인가 보군요!" 첫 번째 경찰관이 소리

치면서, 자신의 권총을 빼 들었습니다.
"손들어, 너희 둘!"

강도들에게 수갑이 채워지는 동안, 다른 경찰차가 달려왔습니다. 램찹 씨가 거기에서 뛰어내렸습니다.

"저 승합차에 달린, 저 풍선!" 그가 외쳤습니다. "우리는 그것을 따라왔어요! 스탠리 . . . ? 너 그 안에 있니?"

"네!" 스탠리가 대답하며 외쳤습니다. "전 괜찮아요. 은행 강도들이 붙잡혔어요! 그들은 전혀 여자가 아니었어요, 단지 그렇게 옷을 입은 것뿐이었어요!"

수갑을 찬 강도들은 굉장히 혼란스러워했습니다. "누가 우리 승합차 안에서 소리 지르는 거지? . . . 누가 문에 풍선을 달아놓은 거야? . . . 우리가 미쳐가는 건가?" 그들이 물었습니다.

"그건 내 아들 스탠리예요." 램찹 씨가 말했습니다. "그는 안타깝게도, 눈에 보이지 않지요. 그가 다치지 않아서 정말 다행이에요!"

"저건 분명 TV에 나왔던 같은 보이지 않는 소년일 거야!" 첫 번째 경찰관이 말했습니다.

"보이지 않는 소년이라고?" 키 큰 강도가 끙 하고 앓는 소리를 냈습니다. "내가 이렇게 조심스러운 계획을 모두 세웠는데!"

통통한 강도가 어깨를 으쓱거렸습니다. "넌 모든 일을 다 생각할 수는 없어,

하워드. 너 자신을 탓하지는 마."

강도들은 교도소로 이송되었고, 스탠리는 램찹 씨와 함께 택시를 타고 집으로 갔습니다.

스탠리가 지나치게 너무 용감하게 굴었다고, 램찹 부인이 그가 무슨 일을 했는지 들었을 때 말했습니다. 정말이지! 그 아이스크림 뚜껑을 뒤집어 열다니! 아서는 자신도 그것들을 뒤집었을 거라고 말했습니다, 만약 그가 그런 생각을 했더라면 말이에요.

7장 아서가 만든 폭풍

램찹 부부는 잘 자라고 인사했습니다. 잠시 형제는 자기 침대에 조용히 누워 있었습니다.

그때 아서가 하품했습니다. "잘 자, 스탠리 형. 좋은 꿈 꿔."

"좋은 꿈을 꾸라고? 하!"

"하?"

"오늘 그 강도들 말이야, 그들은 총을 갖고 있었다고!" 스탠리가 말했습니다. "그들은 실수로 날 쏘았을 수도 있고 그럼 심지어 아무도 몰랐을 거야."

"난 그렇게 생각해 본 적 없었어." 아서가 일어나 앉았습니다. "형 나한테 화났어?"

"그렇지는 않아. 하지만 . . ." 아서가

한숨을 쉬었습니다. "문제는 있지, 나는 계속 보이지 않는 채로 있고 싶지 않아. 나는 오늘 정말 무서웠고, 나는 저 풍선을 들고 다니는 게 싫지만, 내가 그러지 않을 땐, 사람들이 내게 부딪히곤 해. 그리고 나는 거울에 비친 내 모습을 볼 수도 없어서, 나는 내가 어떻게 생겼는지도 기억나지 않아! 마치 내가 납작해졌을 때와 같아. 한동안은 모든 게 괜찮지만, 그러다가 사람들은 나를 비웃었지."

"그게 바로 내가 형을 불어서 다시 둥글게 만든 이유잖아." 아서가 자랑스럽게 말했습니다. "모두 내가 얼마나 똑똑한지에 대해 말했지."

"네가 그렇게 똑똑하다면, 날 이 곤경에서 구해줘!" 스탠리의 목소리가 약간 떨렸습니다.

아서는 가서 자기 형의 침대 끝에 앉았습니다. 이불 아래에 있는 발을 더듬어, 그는 그것을 토닥거렸습니다. "난 정말 형에게 일어난 일에 대해 유감이야." 그가 말했습니다. "난 바라건대—"

문을 두드리는 소리가 났고 램찹 부부가 들어왔습니다. "이야기하는 거니, 너희 둘? 너희는 잠을 자고 있었어야지." 그들이 말했습니다.

아서가 스탠리의 불행한 기분에 대해 설명했습니다.

"게다가 더 있어요." 스탠리가 말했습니다. "두 번이나 제 친구들이 파티를 열었는데 저를 초대하지 않았어요. 그들은 가끔 저를 잊어버리곤 해요. 심지어 제가 계속 풍선을 흔들고 있는데도 말이에요!"

"불쌍한 녀석!" 램찹 부인이 말했습니다. "속담에서 이르기를, '눈에서 보이지 않으면, 마음에서 멀어진다'더니." 그녀가 가서 자신의 팔로 스탠리를 감싸려고 했지만, 그는 방금 침대에서 일어나 앉았고 그녀가 그를 놓치고 말았습니다. 그녀는 그를 찾았고 그를 안아주었습니다.

"이건 끔찍해요!" 아서가 말했습니다. "우리는 무언가를 해야만 해요!"

램찹 씨가 자신의 고개를 저었습니다. "댄 의사 선생님은 스탠리의 상태에 대한 어떤 치료법도 모른단다. 그리고 안 좋은 날씨와 과일 사이에 있는 일말의 관계만을 제외하고는 그 원인에 대해서는 거의 알지도 못하고 말이다."

"그럼 전 늘 이렇게 지내야겠네요." 스탠리의 목소리가 다시 떨렸습니다. "전 나이가 들고 커지겠지만, 누구도 볼 수 없을 거예요."

아서가 생각했습니다. "스탠리 형은 과일을 먹기는 했어요. 그리고 폭풍우가 치기는 했어요. 아마도 . . . 잠깐!"

그가 자신의 아이디어를 설명했습니다.

램찹 부부는 서로를 바라보았고, 그 다음에 스탠리가 있을 거라고 그들이 생각하는 곳을, 그리고 다시 서로를 보았습니다.

"전 두렵지 않아요." 스탠리가 말했습니다. "한번 시도해봐요!"

램찹 씨가 고개를 끄덕였습니다. "나도 그걸 해서 나쁠 건 없을 것 같구나."

"나도 그렇게 생각해요." 램찹 부인이 말했습니다. "아주 좋아, 아서! 네 계획에 필요한 것들을 모아보자!"

"모두 준비됐나요?" 아서가 말했습니다. "그건 스탠리가 보이지 않게 된 밤과 같은 방식이어야만 해요."

"난 같은 파란색-하얀색 줄무늬 잠옷을 입고 있어." 스탠리가 말했습니다. "그리고 난 사과를 갖고 있어. 또 건포도가 든 상자도."

"우리는 진짜 폭풍우는 만들 수 없어요." 아서가 말했습니다. "하지만 아마도 이게 통할 수도 있어요."

그가 욕실로 들어섰고 세면대와 샤워기에 물을 틀었습니다. "저게 비가 되는 거예요." 그가 돌아오면서, 말했습니다. "제가 바람을 맡을게요."

램찹 부인이 부엌에서 가져온 나무 숟가락과 큰 프라이팬을 들어 올렸습니다. "천둥도 준비되었단다." 그녀가 말했습니다.

램찹 씨가 자신의 도구 상자에서 그가 가져온 강력한 손전등을 보여주었습니다. "번개도 준비됐단다."

스탠리가 자신이 든 사과를 들어 올렸습니다. "지금이야?"

"가서 창문 옆에 서." 아서가 말했습니다. "이제 내가 좀 생각해 볼게. 흠... 그날은 어두웠어." 그가 전등을 껐습니다. "어서, 먹어. 휘잉!" 그가 바람이 되어, 덧붙였습니다.

스탠리가 사과를 먹기 시작했습니다.

욕실에서 물이 세면대로, 그리고 샤워기에서 욕조로, 후두두 떨어졌습니다.

"휘잉...휘잉!" 아서가 말했고, 램찹 부인이 그녀의 프라이팬을 나무 숟가락으로 때렸습니다. 그 쾅! 하는 소리는 마치 천둥 같았습니다.

"번개 차례예요." 아서가 말했습니다.

램찹 씨가 자신의 손전등을 겨누었고 그것을 켰다가 끄는 동안 스탠리가 사과를 다 먹었습니다.

"이제 건포도 차례야." 아서가 말했습니다. "한 번에 하나씩 먹어. 휘잉!"

스탠리가 작은 상자를 열었고 건포도를 먹었습니다.

여전히 휘잉 하는 소리를 내면서, 아서는 마치 자기 앞에 오케스트라가 앉아있는 것처럼 지휘했습니다. 그의 왼손으로 램찹 부인에게 프라이팬을 치라고, 오른손으로는 램찹 씨에게 등을 깜박이라고 신호를 보냈습니다. 고개를 끄덕이는 것으로 스탠리에게 언제 건포도를 먹을지 알렸습니다.

후두두 . . . 첨벙 하는 소리를 내며 욕실에서 물이 흘렀습니다. "휘잉!" 아서가 소리 냈습니다. 쾅! 프라이팬이 소리 냈습니다. 번쩍! . . . 번쩍! 등이 작동했습니다.

"만약 누가 지금 우리의 모습을 본다면." 램찹 부인이 조용히 말했습니다, "전 설명하기가 참 난감할 거예요."

스탠리가 자기 몸을 내려다보았습니다. "아무 소용도 없어요." 그가 말했습니다. "전 여전히 눈에 보이지 않아요."

"몸을 비틀어 봐!" 아서가 말했습니다. "어쩌면 이 소음과 빛이 형에게 어떤 방식으로 닿아야 할지도 몰라!"

몸을 비틀면서, 스탠리는 건포도 세 개를 더 먹었습니다. 빛이 그의 몸 위로 깜박거렸습니다. 그는 물이 첨벙거리는 소리를, 아서가 휘잉 하는 소리를 내는 것을, 프라이팬을 숟가락으로 쿵쿵 두들기는 소리를 들었습니다. 그들이 얼마나 열심히 노력하는지 좀 봐, 그가 생각했습니다. 그는 그들을 모두 정말 많이 사랑했어요!

하지만 그는 아직 눈에 보이지 않았지요.

"건포도가 딱 하나만 남았어." 그가 말했습니다. "아무 소용도 없었어."

"가엾은 스탠리!" 램찹 부인이 외쳤습니다.

아서는 다시는 자기 형을 절대로 보지 못 한다는 생각을 견딜 수 없었습니다. "마지막 건포도를 먹어, 스탠리 형." 그가 말했습니다. "먹어 봐!"

스탠리를 건포도를 먹었고 한 번 더 몸을 비틀었습니다. 램찹 부인은 자신의 프라이팬을 두드렸고 램찹 씨는 자신의 손전등을 깜박였습니다. 아서가 마지막으로 휘잉 하는 소리를 냈어요!

아무 일도 일어나지 않았습니다.

"적어도 저는 배고프지는 않아요." 스탠리가 용감하게 말했습니다. "그런데─" 그가 한 손을 자기 뺨에 갖다 대었습니다. "전 . . . 약간 간지러운 기분이 들어요."

"스탠리!" 램찹 씨가 말했습니다. "너 네 뺨을 만지고 있는 거니? 난 네 손이 보이는 것 같구나!"

"그리고 형의 잠옷도!" 아서가 외치면서, 전등을 켰습니다.

흐릿한 줄무늬가 위아래로 뻗은, 일종의 스탠리 램찹의 윤곽이 창가에 나타났습니다. 줄무늬 사이로 그들이 옆집을 볼 수 있기는 했지만.

갑자기 윤곽이 채워졌습니다. 저기 스탠리가, 그들이 그를 기억하던 그 모습대로, 자신의 줄무늬 잠옷을 입고 서 있었습니다!

"전 제 발이 보여요!" 스탠리가 외쳤습니다. "나에요!"

"저라고 해야지, 애야, 나라고 하지 말고." 램찹 부인이 그녀 자신을 말릴 새도 없이 말했고, 그리고는 달려가 그를 꼭 안아주었습니다.

램찹 씨는 아서와 악수했고, 그러고 나서 그들은 모두 욕실로 가서 스탠리가 자신의 모습을 거울에 비춰보는 것을 지켜보았습니다. 램찹 부인이 말하기를, 그가 보이지 않았을 땐 상관없었지만, 그는 정말로 이제 머리카락을 자를 필요가 있다고 했습니다.

그녀는 이 상황을 축하하기 위해 따뜻한 코코아를 만들었고, 모두 아서의 현명함을 인정했습니다.

"하지만 가짜 폭풍우는 믿을 만하지 않지." 램찹 씨가 말했습니다. "우리는 날씨가 좋지 않을 때 과일을 먹기 전에 신중해야만 한단다. 특히 창가에서는 말이야."

그리고는 형제는 다시 잠자리에 들었습니다. "잘 자렴." 램찹 부부가 전등을 끄면서 말했습니다.

"안녕히 주무세요." 스탠리와 아서가 말했습니다.

스탠리가 일어나서 욕실에 있는 거울로 자기 모습을 또 보러 갔습니다. "고마워, 아서." 그가 돌아오면서, 말했습니다. "넌 나를 납작해졌던 것에서도 구해주었고, 이번에 네가 나를 또 구해줬네."

"오, 뭐 . . ." 아서가 하품했습니다. "스탠리 형? 형도 알겠지만, 노력해 봐, 한동안은 *평범하게* 있으려고 말이야."

"그럴게." 스탠리가 말했습니다.

곧 그들은 둘 다 잠이 들었습니다.

끝

Prologue

1. A Stanley Lambchop spoke into the darkness above his bed. "I can't sleep. It's the rain, I think."

2. C "Are you awake, Arthur?" "I am now," said his younger brother. "You woke me."

3. B Stanley fetched an apple from the kitchen and ate it by the bedroom window. The rain had worsened.

4. B Stanley found the little box of raisins on a shelf by the window.

5. D Arthur yawned. "Go to bed. You can't be hungry still." "I'm not, actually." Stanley got back into bed. "But I feel sort of . . . oh, different, I guess."

Chapter 1

1. C "Excuse me," said Arthur. "The thing is, I can hear Stanley, but I can't find him!"

2. B Mr. and Mrs. Lambchop looked about the room. A shape was visible beneath the covers of Stanley's bed, and the pillow was squashed down, as if a head rested upon it. But there was no head.

3. A Stanley got out of bed and put on different pajamas, but these too vanished, reappearing only when he took them off. It was the same with the shirt and trousers he tried on next.

4. D Mrs. Lambchop shook her head. "How are we to keep track of you, dear?" "I know!" said Arthur. Untying a small red balloon, a party favor, that floated above his bed, he gave Stanley the string to hold. "Try this," he said.

5. B The string vanished, but not the balloon.

Chapter 2

1. D "Well, let's have the little fellow in." "I am in," said Stanley, standing directly before him. "Holding the balloon." "Ha, ha, Mr. Lambchop!" said Dr. Dan. "You are an excellent ventriloquist! But I see through your little joke!"

2. A "Headache?" Dr. Dan asked Stanley's balloon. "Throat sore? Stomach

upset?" "I feel fine," Stanley said.

3. D Dr. Dan returned the book to the shelf. "That's it," he said. "Gemeister suspects a connection between bad weather and fruit."

4. B "Why do his clothes also disappear?" "Not my field, I'm afraid," said Dr. Dan. "I suggest a textile specialist."

5. C The red balloon, though useful in locating Stanley, kept reminding them of how much they missed his dear face and smile. But after dinner Mrs. Lambchop, who was artistically talented, replaced the red balloon with a pretty white one and got out her watercolor paints. Using four colors and several delicate brushes, she painted an excellent likeness of Stanley, smiling, on the white balloon.

Chapter 3

1. A Miss Benchley spoke to the class. "We must not stare at where we suppose Stanley to be," she said. "Or gossip about his state."

2. D The headline read: SMILING STUDENT: "ONCE YOU SAW HIM, NOW YOU DON'T!" Beneath it were two photographs, a Before and an After. The Before, taken by Miss Benchley a week earlier, showed a smiling Stanley at his desk.

3. C Arthur said that "Invisible Boy's Brother" would have been an interesting picture, and that Stanley should suggest it if the reporter came around again.

4. B Being invisible offered temptations, Mr. and Mrs. Lambchop warned, but Stanley must resist them. It would be wrong to spy on people, for example, or sneak up on them to hear what they were saying.

5. A Just as the film began, a very tall man sat directly in front of Stanley, blocking his view. Mr. Lambchop took Stanley on his lap, from which the screen was easily seen, and the people farther back saw right through him without knowing it. Stanley greatly enjoyed the show.

Chapter 4

1. C Stanley remembered how nervous he had been when he was learning

to ride and how his father had steadied him. Poor Billy! If only . . . I'll do it! he thought, and tied his balloon to the bench.

2. D "Too bad you missed it, Stanley," said Mr. Lambchop, pretending he had not guessed the truth. "That teetery little boy—he rode very well suddenly." "Oh?" said Stanley, pretending also. "I wasn't paying attention, I guess." Mr. Lambchop gave him a little poke in the ribs.

3. B "That is Phillip, the son of my dear friend Mrs. Hodgson," Mrs. Lambchop said. "And the girl must be his sweetheart, Lucia. Such a sad story! They are in love and Phillip wants very much to propose marriage. But he is too shy. He tries and tries, Mrs. Hodgson says, but each time his courage fails. And Lucia is too timid to coax the proposal from him."

4. D Phillip looked as if he might faint. "What? Did I—? You will?" Lucia hugged him, and they kissed. "I've proposed at last!" cried Phillip. "I can hardly believe I spoke the words!" You didn't, Stanley thought.

5. A Mr. and Mrs. Lambchop had seen the lovers embrace. "Well done, Stanley!" they said when he returned to their bench, and several more times on the way home.

Chapter 5

1. B Stanley said that he did not particularly care to go on TV. But then he remembered about cheering up Arthur. "All right," he said. "But Arthur, too. He likes to tell jokes and do magic tricks. Say we'll both be on the show."

2. C "Invisible Stanley has been delayed but will be here shortly," Teddy Talker told the audience. "Meanwhile, we are fortunate in having with us his very talented brother!" Protests rose. "Brother? . . . A visible brother? . . . Drat! . . . Good thing we got in free!"

3. D "Your card, sir, is the four of hearts!" "It is!" cried Teddy Talker. "It is the four of hearts!" Voices rose again. "Incredible! . . . He can read minds? . . . So young, too! . . . Do that one again, lad!" "Certainly!" said Arthur. But he had used a false deck in which every card was the four of hearts, and the audience

would surely guess if that card was named again.

4. A The audience was tremendously impressed. "What a fine magician! . . . Mind reading and frog flying! . . . You don't see that every day!"

5. C "It wouldn't be fair to let you think I did everything by myself. I had a helper! For the second trick, he saw the card and told me what it was. And Henry . . . Well, my helper was whooshing him in the air!" By now the audience was terribly confused. "Who?" . . . "What helper?" . . . "It was just a regular frog?" . . . "But some frogs fly!" . . . "No, squirrels, not frogs!" . . . "Whooshing?" Arthur went on. "My brother, Stanley, helped me! He fixed it for me to be on this show! He's a really nice brother, and I thank him a lot!"

Chapter 6

1. C Being invisible won't protect me if bullets go flying about! Stanley thought. He looked for a place to hide. An empty Yum-Yum ice cream van was parked close by and he jumped into it.

2. B The robbers were in the van now, close to where he hid. "Hurry up!" said the stout woman in a surprisingly deep voice. "These shoes are killing me!" The tall woman opened the YUM CRUNCH barrel, and Stanley saw that it was empty. Then both robbers poured packets of money from their bags into the barrel and put the lid back on.

3. D "A bank got robbed," the first policeman told the driver. "By two women. You ice-cream fellows seen any suspicious-looking females?" "My!" The tall man shook his head. "More and more these days, women filling roles once played by men. Bless 'em, I say!"

4. A How can I . . . ? An idea came to him. Reaching out, he flipped the lid off the CHOCOLATE YUM barrel. "Loose lid," said the second policeman. "Better tighten— Hey! This barrel is full of female clothes!" "Oh!" The tall robber made a sad face. "For the needy," he said. "They were my late mother's." Stanley flipped the lid off the YUM CRUNCH barrel and the packets of money were plain to see! "Your mother was a mighty rich woman!" shouted the first policeman,

drawing his pistol. "Hands up, you two!"

5. D As the robbers were being handcuffed, another police car drove up. Mr. Lambchop jumped out of it. "That balloon, on that van!" he shouted. "We've been following it! Stanley . . . ? Are you in there?" "Yes!" Stanley called back.

Chapter 7

1. B Stanley sighed. "The thing is, I don't want to go on being invisible. I was really scared today, and I hate carrying that balloon, but when I don't, people bump into me. And I can't see myself in the mirror, so I don't even remember how I look! It's like when I was flat. It was all right for a while, but then people laughed at me."

2. A "Everyone ready?" said Arthur. "It has to be just the way it was the night Stanley got invisible." "I'm wearing the same blue-and-white stripey pajamas," said Stanley. "And I have an apple. And a box of raisins." "We can't make a real storm," Arthur said. "But maybe this will work." He stepped into the bathroom and ran the water in the sink and shower. "There's rain," he said, returning. "I'll be wind."

3. A Mrs. Lambchop held up a wooden spoon and a large skillet from the kitchen. "Thunder ready," she said.

4. C "Twist around!" said Arthur. "Maybe the noise and light have to hit you just a certain way!" Twisting, Stanley ate three more raisins.

5. D "There's only one raisin left," he said. "It's no use." "Poor Stanley!" cried Mrs. Lambchop. Arthur could not bear the thought of never seeing his brother again. "Do the last raisin, Stanley," he said. "Do it!" Stanley ate the raisin and did one more twist. Mrs. Lambchop tapped her skillet and Mr. Lambchop flashed his light. Arthur gave a last Whooosh! Nothing happened. "At least I'm not hungry," Stanley said bravely. "But—" He put a hand to his cheek. "I feel . . . sort of tingly." "Stanley!" said Mr. Lambchop. "Are you touching your cheek? I see your hand, I think!"

투명인간 스탠리
(Invisible Stanley)

1판 1쇄   2017년 9월 4일
2판 2쇄   2024년 7월 15일

지은이   Jeff Brown
책임편집   김보경 정소이
콘텐츠제작및감수   롱테일 교육 연구소
저작권   명채린
마케팅   두잉글 사업 본부

기획   심승규
펴낸이   이수영
펴낸곳   롱테일북스
출판등록   제2015-000191호
주소   04033 서울특별시 마포구 양화로 113, 3층(서교동, 순흥빌딩)
전자메일   team@ltinc.net

ISBN 979-11-91343-62-5 14740